A Guide to Achieving
**AUTONOMOUS
VALUE STREAM FLOW**
with Lean Techniques

Operational
Excellence
in Your Office

A Guide to Achieving
**AUTONOMOUS
VALUE STREAM FLOW**
with Lean Techniques

Operational
Excellence
in Your Office

Kevin J. Duggan with Tim Healey

CRC Press
Taylor & Francis Group
Boca Raton London New York

CRC Press is an imprint of the
Taylor & Francis Group, an **informa** business

A PRODUCTIVITY PRESS BOOK

CRC Press
Taylor & Francis Group
6000 Broken Sound Parkway NW, Suite 300
Boca Raton, FL 33487-2742

© 2016 by Kevin J. Duggan, Tim Healey
CRC Press is an imprint of Taylor & Francis Group, an Informa business

No claim to original U.S. Government works

Printed on acid-free paper
Version Date: 20160113

International Standard Book Number-13: 978-1-4987-1408-2 (Paperback)

Library of Congress Cataloging-in-Publication Data

Duggan, Kevin J.
    Operational excellence in your office : a guide to achieving autonomous value stream flow with lean techniques / Kevin J. Duggan and Tim Healey.
        pages cm
    Includes index.
    ISBN 978-1-4987-1408-2
    1. Organizational effectiveness. 2. Organizational behavior. I. Healey, Tim. II. Title.

HD58.9.D843 2016
658.4'013--dc23   2015010094

Visit the Taylor & Francis Web site at
http://www.taylorandfrancis.com

and the CRC Press Web site at
http://www.crcpress.com

Contents

Introduction

Even as you read this book, there is a fundamental shift going on in the world of continuous improvement. The term *Operational Excellence* is replacing terms like *Lean* and *Continuous Improvement* in the corporate world. Positions that used to be director of Lean, manager of Continuous Improvement, or Lean specialist are now director of Operational Excellence, manager of Operational Excellence, and OpEx specialist. These titles are reflective of the need for a new breed of transformation agents, as well as a new type of change.

That's not the only change. While most Lean and other continuous improvement techniques were born in manufacturing, the concept of Operational Excellence is going far beyond the factory walls. While the director of Lean may have been solely occupied with all matters manufacturing, the new director of Operational Excellence is looking at the entire business. This now means turning attention to the office environment, which has largely been untouched or left alone. Making this move into the office even more challenging is the fact that many companies with an Operational Excellence program are not starting with a bank of experience gained on the manufacturing floor. Hospitals, insurance companies, banks, engineering firms, financial institutions, and more are trying to learn as they go and build that bank of experience and knowledge in their own unique, manufacturing-free environment.

Improvement in the office is not an easy task, even for someone with plenty of experience with continuous improvement tools and Lean techniques. Unlike manufacturing, where inventory moves through the factory, it's hard to see information moving through the office. In the digital age, information is shuffled and moved instantly, not only through the office, but globally, outside the office. It's hard to see, hard to wrap our arms around, and even harder to decide what to do about it. While it's tempting to follow old mantras, such as 5S (workplace organization), kaizen (rapid improvement events), and poka yoke (mistake-proofing) in order to eliminate waste, Operational Excellence demands much more than this. And, in order to achieve Operational Excellence in the office, the approach required is very different. To put it bluntly, *Operational Excellence is not about eliminating waste.*

Rather than focusing on eliminating waste in the pages ahead, we will provide new concepts that create flow in the office. However, not just any flow; a designed flow that "self-heals" when things begin to go wrong. A flow that allows the office to work autonomous*ly without the need for management intervention.* Customers send inquiries to the office, we process the inquiries, and send the customer the response. No management meetings, no oversight, no expedites. It just works day in and day out. Human Resources receives requests to hire new people, they take the request, move the information through their processes, and deliver qualified candidates. Again, no management meetings, no oversight, no expedites. It just works. Engineering has to process engineering changes in a timely manner to support customers and production. Changes are requested, Engineering does the analysis and completes the change. Once again, no management meetings, no oversight, no expedites. It just works.

As titles rapidly change from director of Lean to director of Operational Excellence, the objective is clear—*create self-healing, autonomous flow that does not require management intervention.* How we achieve this objective counts as well. We can't think of it as an endless journey. We must think of it as a journey with a destination. In fact, there is even an "acid test" to check whether or not we have reached the destination, and, like every journey, it helps to have a roadmap. In the pages ahead, you will find just that. Our hope is that you keep this publication with you as a guidebook. We will encourage you to resist the temptation to use traditional improvement tools to go after low-hanging fruit. Instead, follow the process and do the exercises provided to create your roadmap and guide you along the way. Apply the principles and guidelines; design how self-healing, autonomous flow will work in your office; and create an office that provides its services seamlessly to the customer each and every day, on its own, without the need for management intervention.

About the Authors

Kevin J. Duggan has more than 30 years of experience applying advanced Lean techniques to achieve Operational Excellence and is the author of three books on the subject: *Design for Operational Excellence: A Breakthrough Strategy for Business Growth* (McGraw-Hill, 2011), *Creating Mixed Model Value Streams* (Productivity Press, 2002), and *The Office That Grows Your Business: Achieving Operational Excellence in Your Business Processes* (The Institute for Operational Excellence, 2009). A recognized authority on Operational Excellence, Kevin has contributed to publications such as *Industry Week, Aviation Week, Food Engineering, Flow Control, Assembly, Lean Management Journal,* and *Plant Services,* and has appeared on CNN and the Fox Business Network. He is a frequent keynote speaker, master of ceremonies, and panelist at both public and private conferences globally, and he also lectures graduate students in colleges throughout the United States.

In 1998, Kevin founded Duggan Associates (North Kingstown, Rhode Island), an international training and advisory firm that assists companies in applying advanced Lean techniques to their manufacturing and office operations through hands-on support and workshops on topics such as Creating Mixed Model Value Streams, Creating Flow through Shared Resources, Creating Flow through the Supply Chain, Creating Business Process Value Streams, and Lean Product Development. Since Duggan Associates's inception, he has helped Fortune 500 corporations to small businesses with single-site operations in every industry, such as insurance, engineering development, financial services, aerospace, energy, and manufacturing, including United Technologies Corporation, FMC Technologies, Caterpillar, Pratt & Whitney, Singapore Airlines, IDEX Corporation, GKN, and Parker Hannifin. In 2007, Kevin founded the Institute for Operational Excellence (also in North Kingstown), the leading educational center on Operational Excellence, which provides resources, such as workshops, online training, how-to articles, and books to a global community of members.

Tim Healey is a director at Duggan Associates, an international training and advisory firm that assists companies in applying advanced Lean techniques to achieve Operational Excellence. He leads Duggan Associates's complex office environment team, overseeing the teaching and implementing of Operational Excellence principles at global organizations in a wide variety of industries. Tim specializes in helping engineering, product development, human resources, finance, and sales and marketing departments, and has worked with Fortune 500 companies, such as Aetna, FMC Technologies, Parker Hannifin, and United Technologies Corporation. Prior to moving to the United States, Tim worked in the consumer packaged goods industry in Australia, where he held a variety of marketing and sales roles at major Australian and United States organizations.

Acknowledgments

There are several people to thank for their help in developing and applying the principles of Operational Excellence to the office environment. These include the instructors and staff at the Institute for Operational Excellence and Duggan Associates, where these principles are applied throughout the entire office. Special thanks to Abe, Brian, Bruno, Crit, Doug, Edgar, Elisa, Eric, Jennifer, John, Kate, Kirk, Lewis, Liz, Robert D., Robert B., Thomas, Tony, and Tim L. The staff at Duggan Associates and Institute for Operational Excellence use the principles of Operational Excellence each day in the delivery of their respective services to the customer.

I would also like to thank James Marrese for his efforts in putting this work together, as many long days, nights, and weekends were spent by James.

This book was designed by Liz Duggan, to whom I give a special thanks for her hard work. While Liz has done a variety of graphic design projects, this was her first book. Great job Liz!

Tim Healey has been pioneering the concepts in this book with me over the past five years. His work in applying these concepts to engineering, human resources, finance, sales, marketing, product development, and other office areas has provided us with the real life experience that enabled us to shape this work into a very practical application. I cannot thank you enough, Tim!

How to Use This Book

Operational Excellence in Your Office: A Guide to Achieving Autonomous Value Stream Flow with Lean Techniques is written to be a practical guide, so that the reader can learn and apply the techniques taught within its pages in an effort to achieve Operational Excellence in the office.

We have chosen to focus the book's material on designing flow in the office using the nine guidelines for office flow that enable Operational Excellence in the office. Because the focus is on these guidelines and how they apply to your office environment, we will only lightly cover the mechanics of value stream mapping and the icons that make up its underlying language. The nine guidelines will be explained in an easy-to-read manner, with helpful diagrams and illustrations included.

Near the end of each chapter, *action items* will describe the series of activities that should be completed in order to execute and implement the guideline just covered.

Additionally, a *step-by-step checklist* has been provided to assist you in the completion of each action item and also to ensure that the proper methodology is being followed for implementing the specific guideline in question.

Along with each guideline, an *acid test* is also included. This can be used to quickly check whether each guideline has been implemented correctly.

At the end of each chapter, space has been created in the book that can be used to actually complete or sketch how you will implement the guideline covered. We encourage you to take a walk through your office and, based on what you just learned, determine how you would implement the guidelines taught in that chapter. We encourage you to use the actual book as a tool, because it is intended for you to write, draw, and take notes in as you walk through your office and accomplish each task.

In order to assist in applying the nine guidelines for office flow, we also provide examples of how each guideline would apply to different office environments. Specifically, we provide examples on how each guideline would apply to human resources (HR) and engineering. Look for these examples at the end of each chapter under the heading "Practical Application."

The HR and engineering applications are just samples of what can be done in the office. The guidelines are applicable in all office functions. They are equally as powerful when deployed in departments such as finance, accounting, legal, marketing, sales, organizational development, treasury, and other office areas where we provide a service to the customer or another area of the business by processing information.

By following the methodology in this book, you will not only learn the step-by-step process for creating flow in the office, but also how to achieve true Operational Excellence in a practical manner. The result is much more than a waste-free, efficient office. It is an office that can be leveraged to drive top-line revenue and business growth.

With this in mind, we hope you use this book as a workbook to guide you along the way. Please write in it, draw sketches, and share the exercises with others in order to take them with you as you begin your journey to Operational Excellence in the office. Now it's time to get started.

part
one
Getting Started

chapter
one

Operational Excellence in the Office

Throughout the years, many different ways to improve the office have been developed, most of them typically focused on project management software, ERP (enterprise resource planning) systems, database improvements, new computer systems, and, lately, using Lean techniques in the office in order to eliminate waste. Operational Excellence, however, is different from these methods right from the very first step, which is focused on *designing how the office should operate and function day in and day out.*

To do this, we design how information will flow through the office from when a request for a service is initialized, through all of the activities required to process the request, and on to when the service is delivered to the customer. Principles and guidelines are used to design this flow of information correctly and in a way that enables the on-time delivery of the service to the customer in a repeatable manner.

When flow is designed using the principles and guidelines of Operational Excellence, it results in an office where information flows from activity to activity along fixed pathways at preset, predefined times. Everyone knows what to work on next from the designed flow, not from managers setting priorities and making decisions. Everyone in the office knows where they get their work from, when to expect the information they need, and when to send their completed work to the next activity in the flow. The design guidelines also describe how information will ultimately be delivered to the customer, how we will respond to the customer, and, most importantly, create a *guaranteed turnaround time* for when the service will be delivered to the customer once it has been requested each and every time.

While these are the immediate results of designing an office based on the principles and guidelines of Operational Excellence, the true intent of applying the design guidelines is much deeper. Designing how the office will operate and deliver its service to the customer allows us to define the normal manner in which information flows and the service is provided, in other words, *normal flow*. By doing this, we also define when something begins to go wrong with the delivery of the service and abnormalities occur—*abnormal flow*. This is a critical element of Operational Excellence. No matter how robustly we design the normal flow for a service, things *will* go wrong. It's what we do when things go wrong that counts.

The Need for Management Intervention

Typically, when things go wrong in the office and there is an abnormal condition, the flow of information and work slows down or comes to a halt. To correct the problem, management intervenes and attempts to give direction on what can be done to fix the problem. This process is not always quick, and there is no guarantee that the response given is the correct one needed to resume normal flow. Management has to acquire information, determine what the issue is and its causes and effects, and discuss the issue via emails and phone calls with other management personnel who might be occupied with other tasks and not have availability.

Eventually, if the issue does not get resolved or to bring more awareness to the issues, management calls a meeting. The purpose of the meeting is to resolve the issue that is either negatively affecting the customer at present or that will do so if nothing is done. After much debate, negotiation, bargaining, and, often, more meetings, a corrective decision is ultimately made and implemented to fix the abnormal flow and resume the normal flow of work and information to the customer. This takes quite a bit of management time, effort, and coordination to resolve the issue and get the service to the customer. In fact, in many companies, it's a full-time position.

In achieving Operational Excellence in the office, this is where the contrast lies. Once achieved, there is no need for endless emails, meetings, or status updates. Management intervention is greatly reduced, along with all of the coordination efforts and the hours spent each day "managing" the services we provide in the office. In fact, Operational Excellence can eliminate the need for management intervention almost entirely. Instead, the office runs *autonomously*, delivering the service day in and day out by self-correcting when abnormalities occur, allowing management to spend its time on activities that grow the business, or *offense* activities.

How is the need for management intervention virtually eliminated? It's not done by strong leaders who drive people to improve. It's done by following a methodology or process. The key is to design how information should flow to the customer using principles and guidelines rather than seeking to eliminate waste through brainstorming or kaizen (rapid improvement) activities. There are places where we will use brainstorming and kaizen activities in Operational Excellence, but we do not use them in the design phase.

Once we have designed the flow of information through the office, and thereby defined normal and abnormal flow, the next step is to make those flow conditions *visible*. This means that anyone in the office, and even a visitor, would be able to walk the flow from beginning to end and identify whether the service provided is proceeding normally or abnormally. This is known as the "acid test" for Operational Excellence: Bring a visitor into your office and see if he/she can tell if it is on time for the service it provides. After all, if a visitor can tell if the service is on time, then so can the people who work there, including, most importantly, those who work directly in the flow.

With a designed flow implemented, along with visuals in place that tell us if the flow is normal or abnormal, we can teach the employees who work in the flow how to recognize when abnormal conditions have occurred and what can be done to correct them. This creates *self-healing value streams* (which is a key concept in Operational Excellence) in the office that flow work and information seamlessly and autonomously to the customer, which eliminates the need for management intervention.

In an office that achieves Operational Excellence, managers no longer need to spend time creating status updates, attending meetings, or chasing emails and voicemails. They now spend their time focusing squarely on the activities that grow the business, such as meeting with customers, meeting with *potential* customers, focusing exclusively on the voice of the customer (VOC), and innovating new products and services with customers. Additionally, the organizational chart has very few positions dedicated to the oversight and delivery of the service to the customer because it just works autonomously day in and day out. The end result of an office that has achieved Operational Excellence is the ability to *leverage your office for business growth*, which means your office has a strategic advantage in capturing new business and increasing market share faster than competitors, both immediately and well into the future.

Applying Lean Concepts to the Office

In 1996, the book *Lean Thinking*[1] was published, and it started a movement to improve mostly manufacturing operations through the identification and elimination of waste. Over time, this thinking migrated to the office, as significant gains were made in manufacturing, and organizational leaders correctly saw that major opportunities existed in the office for similar advances. These techniques, often referred to as "Lean techniques," have been highly successful, but there is a difference in how these techniques are applied to achieve Operational Excellence in the office.

Traditional Lean applications typically follow this process (for more information, see Appendix D):

1. Management sees an area where performance is lacking in the office.

2. A cross-functional team is issued goals and tasked with improving the area.

3. The team creates a current state map that depicts how the office delivers a service to the customer.

4. Opportunities for improvement are identified through kaizen (rapid improvement) bursts.

5. Lean tools, such as kaizen, mistake proofing, problem solving, and others, are used to execute the improvements.

6. Once implemented, the improvements are adopted through standard work.

7. The results are measured and monitored and corrections are made if needed.

8. Management moves on to another area of the office where performance is lacking to begin the cycle again.

These traditional techniques make incremental gains over many years, and the improvements are considered to be along a journey, an endless journey of waste elimination. When asked about the improvements, when they will be done, and where they will take the company, the answer is commonly: "It's about the journey. There is no destination."

The OpEx Difference

While still using the Lean tools of value stream mapping and other Lean techniques, the concept of Operational Excellence in the office is a much more progressive approach to improvement. Rather than an endless journey of waste elimination, we will *set a destination* of where our improvement efforts will take us.

It's important to note that this destination is not described in terms of results, management goals or objectives, or company financial measurements. The destination is described in terms of what each employee would see with his/her eyes and hear with his/her ears when walking through the office. The intent with this destination is not to give a vision or direction (such as "eliminate waste"), but to describe a state of performance for the office that everyone can recognize has been achieved.

This state has to be achievable in all areas of the organization, teachable to all levels of the organization, and *actionable*. By actionable, we mean every employee in the organization can actually *use* the destination to know what their work area would look and be like; how their area would operate, function, and perform every day; and whether their area was getting to or had achieved the destination, or if more work still needed to be done. A good, practical destination that meets the needs of all of our Lean and continuous improvement efforts is the very definition of Operational Excellence. Operational Excellence is when:

Each and every employee can see the flow of value to the customer, and fix that flow before it breaks down.^{SM}

Using this definition of Operational Excellence as the destination for all of our continuous improvement efforts provides a tangible destination for all areas of the organization. It is practical, applicable, and, most importantly, teachable. By using principles and guidelines, we can teach how information is designed to flow in the office and how each and every employee should be able to see that flow. We can create and teach standard work for that flow as well as standard work for when things go wrong. We can teach that success comes when the flow becomes self-healing and autonomous and eliminates the need for management intervention to deliver the product or service to the customer. We can teach this concept whether the service provided in the office spans one or two people or involves multiple sites distributed across the globe. We also can teach the benefits of Operational Excellence and what it means to each employee in the office. These benefits include:

- The elimination of many meetings, including status meetings, update meetings, management meetings, and any meetings that involve scheduling or prioritizing work.

- The elimination of expedites and management priority changes.

- The elimination of firefighting in order to get the service completed.

- The elimination of competing for resources that are needed to provide the service.

- A large reduction in emails being sent and received.

- A large reduction in the time spent writing and reading emails.

- The elimination of phone calls and emails to clarify work.

- Eliminating the need for and time spent on chasing information.

- Eliminating the need to spend time "filling in the boss."

- Eliminating the need for management oversight.

- Reductions in interruptions that prevent work from being completed.

- Having a productive environment.

- Having a sense of accomplishment each day.

Having a practical definition of Operational Excellence that means something to each and every employee is key. It enables each employee to understand what his/her respective environment will look like when the destination is achieved. It lets each employee know what he/she is trying to accomplish with his/her improvement efforts. And, with every employee knowing this, the office transforms quickly to a self-healing, autonomous flow in months versus the traditional continuous improvement effort that is a never-ending journey.

The Principles of Operational Excellence

To achieve Operational Excellence and become a high-performance office, one not only needs a destination, but a roadmap as well. The combination of a destination and a roadmap allows us to make significant improvement to the office as a whole in a short amount of time. Creating this roadmap involves implementing a specific set of principles that will make Operational Excellence a reality in the office and everywhere in the organization. There are eight principles of Operational Excellence and they must be applied in order[2]:

1. Design Lean value streams.

2. Make Lean value streams flow.

3. Make flow visual.

4. Create standard work for flow.

5. Make abnormal flow visual.

6. Create standard work for abnormal flow.

7. Have employees in the flow improve the flow.

8. Perform offense activities.

We will provide a brief synopsis of the principles as follows and spend a little more time on number eight at the end:

1. **Design Lean value streams:** This is where the difference between traditional Lean and Lean that achieves Operational Excellence begins. Within this principle, there are nine guidelines for office flow, and we will cover them in detail in this book. These nine guidelines are crucial to the success of any transformation and must be given sufficient time and attention.

2. **Make Lean value streams flow:** This means going from "paper to performance," where the design of flow created on paper using the guidelines is made a reality in the organization. In this phase, we educate and engage the employees on how flow is designed to work in their respective areas and work with them to create that flow.

3. **Make flow visual:** The ultimate goal is to make the flow in the office so visual that someone who has never been to the office before could walk the flow from end-to-end without escort and tell if our services in the office are on time just by observing the flow in action.

4. **Create standard work for flow:** This is not simply standard work for how each person performs their work in the office. It is also standard work for how work flows between the processes and for the connections that link the employees in the office together in flow.

5. **Make abnormal flow visual:** This means developing the ability to physically see abnormal flow when things have gone wrong. If a visitor were to walk through the office unescorted, he/she would be able to know if the flow had broken down at any process or process connection, why it had broken down, and the severity of the breakdown.

6. **Create standard work for abnormal flow:** Develop standardized responses for how to correct abnormal flow conditions. This would include standardized methods of response based on logic charts and formalized procedures. A "Plan B" would be developed here, and each employee would know what Plan B is.

7. **Have employees in the flow improve the flow:** Associates at every level of the organization work to design and improve their flow so it lasts well into the future by ensuring the visual indicators and standard work remain robust for both normal and abnormal flow. A good metric for this principle is to measure how many times management must intervene to correct the flow, or a "management intervention" graph.

Once the first seven principles of Operational Excellence have been completed, the organization is ready to commence with the eighth and final principle in earnest, as it is here that the true power of Operational Excellence is revealed.

The Eighth Principle: Perform Offense Activities

When high-performance organizations successfully implement the first seven principles of Operational Excellence, management and company leadership are able to spend their time on offense, or the *activities that grow the business.* Drilling down farther into this concept, offense activities can be divided into long-term and short-term. Certain offense activities result in an immediate return to the business, perhaps in less than three months, such as working with a customer on a new promotion that will showcase the services you provide. Other offense activities may take longer, such as developing new products and services, but the activity still focuses on business growth and offense.

In a high-performance organization, however, it's not just management that works on offense. Achieving Operational Excellence means that employees at *every* level of the organization work on offense. Each employee thinks about his or her tasks and how these duties can assist in business growth and the execution of company strategy. This could be a sales assistant having more time to spend on researching his/her customer's business to provide more powerful insight for the sales manager to present to the customer. It could be a line worker thinking about how difficult it is to assemble the product and the impact that disassembly and reassembly has in the field, the result of which is suggestions for new ways to assemble the product and a competitive advantage over other products in terms of field service.

The intent of achieving Operational Excellence is for each employee to spend all of his or her time on offense activities. With Operational Excellence in place, very little time will be spent on defense, or on fixing flow problems, or on maintenance, which are activities that must be done to maintain the business, such as completing compliance reporting to the government.

In a high-performance office that has applied the first seven principles of Operational Excellence and created self-healing autonomous flow, employees throughout the office will be working on offense more and more. The result is an office that can be leveraged for business growth.

Operational Excellence: Practical Terms

While we have provided the principles of Operational Excellence, there is a practical way to describe it, and this is through the eyes and ears as you walk through the office. Imagine yourself walking through the office. What would you see with your eyes, what would you be hearing with your ears? In an office that has achieved Operational Excellence, you would be able to walk through the office and *see* if the service that the office provides is on time, without asking any questions. You would *hear* people performing the work required to deliver the service. You would not see any meetings to prioritize work, status updates, or management meetings, nor would you hear any firefighting, reprioritizations, interruptions, expedites, or panic. The office would be calm.

Achieving Operational Excellence in the office also means that every employee could easily tell if the flow of the service is normal or abnormal. They also would know what to do when the flow becomes abnormal, and this does not mean that people would hold meetings or begin to seek out supervisors to determine what to do next. Employees would simply consult their standard work for abnormal flow, fix the flow when or even before it breaks down, and then resume operating under normal conditions once the abnormal flow has been fixed. Even when abnormalities happen, the office would be calm.

Another way to describe Operational Excellence in practical terms is to say that the office becomes uneventful. Customers send us orders or requests, we process the work, and send them the information, and it's all uneventful. It's uneventful because it's designed to work this way: no stress, no management interventions, no interruptions, no meetings for status updates, no meetings to fix problems—just meetings focused on business growth. Imagine your office like this. Now imagine it happening in a just a few months. Following the process and performing the exercises in the upcoming pages will get you well on your way.

References

1. Womack, J. P., and D. T. Jones. 1996. *Lean Thinking: Banish Waste and Create Wealth in Your Corporation.* New York: Simon and Schuster.

2. Duggan, K. J. 2011. *Design for Operational Excellence: A Breakthrough Strategy for Business Growth.* New York: McGraw Hill.

chapter
two

The Key Function of Any Office

If you walk out into your workplace and look at everyone working on different tasks, ask yourself one question: How does everyone in the office know what to work on next? Typical answers include via phone calls, emails, meetings, task lists, what the boss says, or, most likely, whatever they feel like working on. With so many ways to choose what to work on at each place where work is performed, connecting processes together in an attempt to create flow would be impossible. To overcome this, we have to change our thinking about the office, and it starts right with understanding the true function of any workplace.

In Operational Excellence, the true function of any office is to *flow information* and *capture knowledge*. It's that simple.

Flowing information means setting a predictable cadence for moving information between people, departments, suppliers, or customers. The end result of this flow is a deliverable to the customers in the form that they need it, such as a report, quote, or spreadsheet, or it might even be the delivery of a product, such as an insurance plan.

A well-designed office also should be capturing the knowledge generated by its processes at set points in the flow for future use, either for the same customer or different ones. This knowledge can be captured in forms or cataloged in component designs, structural support data for products, trade-off curves for product development, and so on. The key is that we understand *where* we will capture knowledge formally so it can be used in the future.

While every office is different, as are the services and capabilities they deliver, they all fulfill these two key functions of *flowing information* and *capturing knowledge*. Therefore, we need to create a system of flow capable of executing these two key tasks and achieving Operational Excellence. The result of this system will be an environment where everyone knows from the flow what to work on next, not from meetings, phone calls, emails, or management decisions.

To create this system, we will use a process to design value stream flow in the office. Remember, this is not your typical value stream mapping technique where we make a current state map, look for opportunities, and run kaizen or rapid improvement events. This is a structured value stream design process that uses guidelines to design the future state. It's through these guidelines that we can teach the future state design, know if the design is working and flow is normal or abnormal, and achieve Operational Excellence in the office.

chapter three

Value Stream Design for the Office

The first principle in achieving Operational Excellence in the office is to design Lean value streams. There is a process to do this, and that process consists of five major steps. From a high level, they include:

1. Determine service families.

2. Create a current state value stream map for each service family.

3. Apply the nine guidelines for office flow.

4. Create the future state value stream map.

5. Create an implementation plan.

Following is a brief summary of each step.

1. **Determine service families:** Service families are created in order to group together services that are provided in the office based on similarity in processing steps and total work content. These groupings can greatly reduce the variation of workflow by looking at individual tasks through many different areas and creating a family of tasks that flow through common areas. A good service family matrix allows us to know where we will be able to create a smooth, stable flow of information and where some of the flows might be more erratic and therefore require different techniques.

2. **Create a current state value stream map for each service family:** Each current state value stream map follows the flow of *one* service family. It depicts the current state of how information flows and how knowledge is captured. It also depicts the total amount of lead time required to deliver the service and compares it to the work time or process time that is required to actually perform the service. (See Appendix A for a more in-depth look at current state maps.)

3. **Apply the nine guidelines for office flow:** There are nine guidelines for
    creating self-healing, autonomous flow in the office and they must be
    followed in sequence. These nine guidelines teach us techniques to
    match output to customer demand, balance work, connect processes,
    put predictable and repeatable timing into the office, capture knowledge,
    sequence work, tell if the office is on time, see if something is wrong,
    and react to changing customer demand. They are critical to the success
    of Operational Excellence in the office.

4. **Create the future state value stream map:** The future state value
    stream map is created by interrogating the current state with the nine
    guidelines. As we learn each guideline, we mock-up and note how we
    could apply it on the current state. After the mock-up is complete,
    make a clean future state that clearly shows the application of the nine
    guidelines along with how we will flow information and capture
    knowledge. The future state also will show the new resultant lead time
    to the customer compared to the process or work time required.
    There is usually a significant difference when the current state is
    compared to the future state. (See Appendix B for a more in-depth look
    at future state maps.)

5. **Create an implementation plan:** The implementation plan is created by
    drawing loops around "areas of flow" depicted on the future state map,
    with each loop containing a list of tasks that need to be accomplished
    in order to fully apply the appropriate guidelines. Dates also would be
    applied to these tasks as per a typical project plan. The implementation
    plan usually starts at the loop closest to the delivery end of the value
    stream. Then, working back upstream, the other loops are implement-
    ed in sequence. Work can be done in multiple areas at the same time.
    However, it is important that the physical connections between the loops
    happen in sequence starting from the loop closest to the delivery of the
    service and then working upstream. (See Appendix C for a more in-depth
    look at implementation plans.)

Of the five major steps to designing Lean value streams for the office, this practical guide will focus on the two that are the most challenging: *determine service families* and *the nine guidelines for office flow*. A review of the remaining steps will be provided in Appendices A, B, and C.

1. Determine service families.

2. Create a current state value stream map for each service family (Appendix A).

3. Apply the nine guidelines for office flow.

4. Create the future state value stream map (Appendix B).

5. Create an implementation plan (Appendix C).

Let's get started with the first step in the value stream design process: determine service families.

chapter
four

Determine Service Families

The first step in the value stream design process is to determine service families, which helps us to understand the similarity of the work that is done in the office and the scope of our value stream design and implementation.

To determine service families, the first step is to identify the potential flows that exist and then formalize them using a specific methodology. A service family should result in the delivery of a service to an external customer or another area of the business and its starting and ending points must be clearly identified. An example of a service family may be providing quotes to a customer (external) or hiring new employees (internal).

A unique tool called a service family matrix is used in order to determine the potential service families that exist within the office. A service family matrix helps identify which services or office capabilities can potentially be grouped into families. It also gives some clear rules as to how service families should be determined and provides a consistent and repeatable approach to scoping that can be understood and applied company-wide.

To create a service family matrix, consider the services or capabilities provided along with the activities required to complete them. We would then create a grid and list the services provided down the left-hand side and the activities across the top (Figure 4.1).

Definition
· ·

A **service family** is
group of services
that go through
similar activities and have
similar work content.

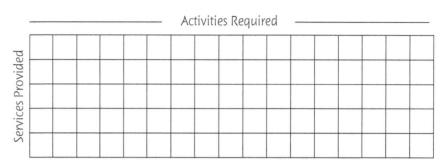

Figure 4.1 **A service family matrix lists the services provided by the office down the left-hand side and the activities required to deliver them across the top.**

Scoping the Matrix

It is not necessary to list all the services and capabilities provided by the entire office, as this would be overwhelming. It is very important that we scope down the matrix to areas we can affect and implement. For example, we would not want to look at a process that has a large portion of its work completed by other sites or divisions, possibly in other countries, because a lot of what goes on will be out of our control. These can certainly be done, but they are a bit more complicated and not ideal for a team's first transformation.

Instead, try starting small with a group of services provided by a functional area and see what that brings, then expand it out to the neighboring areas that provide the inputs and outputs necessary to complete the service. Look for where the service is initialized and how this happens. Specifically, try to find a point where a physical method is used for the initialization, e.g., a formal request, and do the same thing for the completion of the service, e.g., a quote is sent by email to the customer (Figure 4.2 and Figure 4.3).

Once we have the initial breadth of our matrix that shows where the service is initialized and delivered, we then would begin to think in terms of the activities needed to complete the services and list the activities along the top of the grid. When listing the activities performed, try to think of the

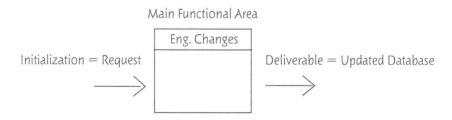

Figure 4.2 **Begin with a primary functional area when creating matrices.**

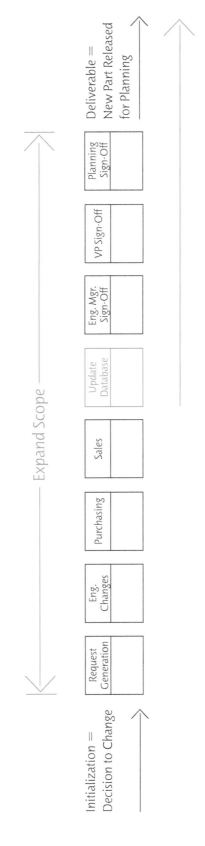

Figure 4.3 **Expand the scope, using the physical initialization and completion of the service as new boundaries.**

specific actions, or verbs, that must occur or be completed in order to deliver the service or capability to the customer. In other words, don't list employ-ees, departments, or functionalities along the top. It is strictly the activities or actual work involved in providing the service or capability to the customer.

To help understand what we mean by activities, think about when work is being done versus when the work is waiting. An easy way to do this is by imagining a "red sticky dot" on the document or information that is being processed and observing where the red sticky dot stops. If you work on something then email it to someone, the red sticky dot stops after you send it, because it will sit in someone else's inbox. The work that happens between the time you begin and the time it is emailed to someone else would comprise the activity that would be listed in the service family matrix (Figure 4.4).

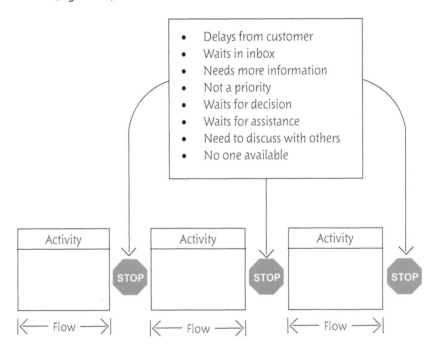

Figure 4.4 **Activities for the service family matrix are defined by where flow starts and stops. In between these areas of flow, information and inventory accumulate.**

Refining the Scope

A service family matrix may initially look like the one seen in Figure 4.5. Services or capabilities that are provided are listed down the left-hand side, while the activities required to perform those services and capabilities are listed across the top. Simply move along the rows that contain each service and mark an "X" where an activity is performed to deliver that service to the customer. Do this for every service provided and activity performed until the entire grid is completed (Figure 4.5).

Services Provided \ Activities Performed	Request Generation	Order Entry	Eng. Verify	Estimate	Purchasing Check	Sales Review	Access Data Whse.	Verify Materials	Sign-Off	Complete Package	VP Sign-Off	Schedule w/ Div. Project Planning
Part Number Change	X	X					X	X	X		X	X
Packaging Change	X	X					X	X	X		X	X
Color Change	X	X		X					X	X	X	X
Material Change	X	X	X	X	X		X	X	X	X	X	X
New Application	X	X	X	X	X	X	X	X	X	X	X	X

Figure 4.5 **A service family matrix containing many services and activities.**

Services Provided \ Activities Performed	Request Generation	Order Entry	Eng. Verify	Estimate	Purchasing Check	Sales Review	Access Data Whse.	Verify Materials	Sign-Off	Complete Package	VP Sign-Off	Schedule w/ Div. Project Planning
Part Number Change	X	X					X	X	X		X	X
Packaging Change	X	X					X	X	X		X	X
Color Change	X	X		X					X	X	X	X
Material Change	X	X	X	X	X		X	X	X	X	X	X
New Application	X	X	X	X	X	X	X	X	X	X	X	X

Figure 4.6 **The service family matrix scoped down.**

Definition

A **natural break in flow** is when:

- Large amounts of information or data have to be moved from one area of the company to another.

- Information has to be sent outside the company for external review or input (e.g., to a supplier or customer).

- A decision is required by someone outside of the defined service family.

Even after some initial scoping, we may find that the matrix is too large and involves too many activities for the initial implementation. In these instances, we would need to scope it down again to something more manageable. In the final scope-down, look closely at where there are natural breaks in flow and what areas we can control.

Considering the span of control is important, because it's necessary to scope the matrix to areas we can impact. In Figure 4.6, for instance, "Request Generation" happens unpredictably based on the varying criteria of individual managers. Therefore, there is not a natural flow from "Request Generation" to "Order Entry."

The final two activities, "VP Sign-Off" and "Schedule with Divisional Project Planning," are part of another division, so they would be excluded because they are out of our span of control for the initial design and implementation (Figure 4.6).

Even though some activities will be omitted in Figure 4.6, they cannot simply be forgotten. Eventually, they will need to be connected into the overall flow. As we will discover, there will be guidelines to help us do this.

Using the Matrix: The 80/30 Guideline

Once the matrix has been fully populated and appropriately scoped, it's time to look for similarities in the activities required to complete the different services. As a general guideline, look for roughly 80 percent similarity in the activities performed among the different services. When different services share roughly 80 percent of the same activities, it means that 80 percent of the information will go through the same physical pathways (even if these are electronic) through the office. With an 80 percent similarity, they can potentially be grouped into a service family. We may find we cannot meet the 80 percent criteria, because the similarities are just not there. If this is the case, we can still apply the guidelines. However, there will be some adjustments required to handle the higher degree of variation. Either way, it will be important to note how much variation exists in the different pathways on which information needs to flow for each potential family. A sorted service family matrix can be seen in Figure 4.7.

Helpful Hint

For matrices that are large or have many processing steps, it might be easier to create the service family matrix electronically.

Services Provided / Activities Performed	Order Entry	Eng. Verify	Estimate	Purchasing Check	Sales Review	Access Data Whse.	Verify Materials	Sign-Off	Complete Package
A Part Number Change	X					X	X	X	
A Packaging Change	X					X	X	X	
B Color Change	X		X					X	X
C Material Change	X	X	X	X		X	X	X	X
C New Application	X	X	X	X	X	X	X	X	X

Figure 4.7 **The matrix sorted into three different service families.**

Services Provided / Activities Performed	Order Entry	Eng. Verify	Estimate	Purchasing Check	Sales Review	Access Data Whse.	Verify Materials	Sign-Off	Complete Package	Total
A Part Number Change	5 min.					10 min.	15 min.	30 min.		**60 min.**
A Packaging Change	5 min.					12 min.	9 min.	20 min.		**46 min.**
B Color Change	5 min.		5 min.					45 min.	35 min.	**90 min.**
C Material Change	5 min.	8 min.	12 min.	10 min.		15 min.	30 min.	10 min.	20 min.	**110 min.**
C New Application	5 min.	8 min.	12 min.	15 min.	15 min.	20 min.	30 min.	15 min.	25 min.	**145 min.**

Figure 4.8 **The matrix with the "Xs" replaced with process times.**

Definition

....

Total work content is defined as how much actual work is involved in providing the service in terms of time. Think of it as if one person performed the entire sequence of activities without any handoffs, waiting, or delays, and had all of the information he needed right when he needed it.

In Figure 4.7, there are three potential service families, each of which has been boxed off with a different color and labeled A, B, and C, respectively. All of the services that fall within each box would be a part of the same service family. For example, the *Material Change* and *New Application* services would both be part of the same service family. Remember, a current state value stream map must be created for each service family identified in the matrix. This would mean that *one* current state map would be created for both the *Material Change* and *New Application* services that this office provides.

Having done this 80 percent grouping, the next step is to further refine our choices by looking at the variation in total work content within the potential service family.

As a guideline, the variation of the total work content time for all the services in a potential family should not exceed 30 percent. By adding this criteria, we can "tune" the family tighter according to work that follows the same pathway and also takes roughly the same amount of time in total. This helps make the output of the work more consistent and predictable by family. If the variation exceeds 30 percent, we can still create flow, but, again, we will need to make adjustments in operating the value stream to allow for the higher variation in time needed.

To determine the variation in the total work content times for the services in a potential family, replace each "X" with the time it takes to complete each activity (the process time) as if only one person did it, then add up the times in each row (Figure 4.8).

To determine the variation in work content, subtract the lowest time *in the family* from the highest time *in the family*, and then divide the result by the highest time *in the family*. This will provide the variation between the highest and lowest times in the service family.

(Highest – Lowest)/Highest

If this equation is applied to service family C, for example, the following answer is generated:

Helpful Hint

....

While we have provided a 30 percent guideline, it is not a magic number. Think the smaller variation, the more consistent flow we will have, no matter what service in the family is required. The higher the number, the more flexibility we will need in running the designed flow, depending on what exact services are required in the family.

145 min. − 110 min. = 35 min.

35 min./145 min. = 0.24, or 24%

The variation is under 30 percent, so this service family checks out okay. Service family C, the *Material Change* and *New Application* services, would now be one value stream.

Service Families and Value Streams

Teams working on transforming an office to Operational Excellence should perform this 80/30 analysis for all potential families identified in the service family matrix. **The aim is to create end-to-end value stream flow for each service family determined.** This means that each family would require a current state map, the application of the nine guidelines, a designed future state, and an implementation plan.

It's possible you may discover that, after performing your service family analysis using the methodology described in this chapter, the families previously mapped in the office were not the right ones needed to establish true office flow. If this is the case, it would be a good idea to redo the current state map using the newly created service families. (See Appendices A, B, and C for more detailed information on this overall process.)

practical application **Human Resources Service Families**

Human Resources (HR) is responsible for providing the organization with many different services and capabilities. The department hires new employees, determines compensation packages, orients and trains new and existing employees, administers company benefits, provides healthcare plan choices, manages pension or retirement options, and much, much more.

With a high number of activities performed and services provided in HR, an initial scoping must be done up front to determine the different services it

Helpful Hint

If the variation exceeded 30 percent, you could try to remove one service from the family (the one with either the highest total work content time or the lowest) and see if the numbers recalculated are under 30 percent. In some instances, it might not be possible to do this, as there might be nowhere else in the office where this activity can be performed.

provides. Because one primary function of HR is hiring new employees, this can serve as a rough scope to begin with, then adjusted with a refined scoping once we know the detailed activities involved.

The *Hire New Employees* service family could potentially encompass several different hiring processes depending on the role that needs to be filled, and the service family matrix will help analyze these differences.

Here are some examples of different hiring requests that come into HR:

- Senior executives

- Managers

- Engineers

- IT (information technology)

- Research and development

These will be listed on the left side of the matrix. On the top of the matrix, we will list the activities or the work required to hire for these positions. Remember, when deciding what an activity is, look for where flow starts and stops and inventory or information accumulates. We are not looking at the people who perform the work, but instead how the work itself moves through the office. We should also do our best to list the activities in sequence as they occur. If an activity is repeated, show it twice on the matrix; do not show it as a "loop back."

Figure 4.9 shows a matrix for some of the positions that HR is responsible for filling.

With the rough scope completed, it can be expanded or reduced based on natural breaks in flow and also by span of control (Figure 4.10).

Helpful Hint

Avoid the trap of assuming service families are dictated by common traits, such as the work performed by a particular department, the required employee skill sets, customer teams, product lines, groupings by marketing or sales, or a range of other options. These traditional methods of grouping processes can make creating flow and achieving Operational Excellence in the office very difficult, if not impossible. When they are used, eventually anything implemented degrades back to management dictating priorities.

	Collect Specifications for New Hire	Submit Formal Request	Candidate Search	Contact Recruiter	Review Resume	First Interview	Evaluate Prior Research	Technical Test 1	Technical Test 2	Technical Test 3	Evaluate Test Results	Review First Interview Results	Second Interview	Review Second Interview Results	Vice President Interview	Review VP Interview Results	C-Suite Interview	Review C-Suite Interview Results	Final Interview	Review Final Interview Results	Configure Compensation Package	Create Offer Letter	Schedule Orientation
Managers	X	X	X		X	X						X	X	X	X	X			X	X	X	X	X
Engineers	X	X	X		X	X		X			X	X	X	X					X	X	X	X	X
R&D	X	X	X	X	X	X	X	X	X	X	X	X	X	X					X	X	X	X	X
Senior Executives	X	X	X		X	X						X	X	X	X	X	X	X	X	X	X	X	X
IT	X	X	X		X	X		X	X		X	X	X	X					X	X	X	X	X

Figure 4.9 **An unsorted matrix for the hiring of employees, a service Human Resources is responsible for providing.**

	Collect Specifications for New Hire	Submit Formal Request	Candidate Search	Contact Recruiter	Review Resume	First Interview	Evaluate Prior Research	Technical Test 1	Technical Test 2	Technical Test 3	Evaluate Test Results	Review First Interview Results	Second Interview	Review Second Interview Results	Vice President Interview	Review VP Interview Results	C-Suite Interview	Review C-Suite Interview Results	Final Interview	Review Final Interview Results	Configure Compensation Package	Create Offer Letter	Schedule Orientation
Managers	X	X	X		X	X						X	X	X	X	X			X	X	X	X	X
Engineers	X	X	X		X	X		X			X	X	X	X					X	X	X	X	X
R&D	X	X	X	X	X	X	X	X	X	X	X	X	X	X					X	X	X	X	X
Senior Executives	X	X	X		X	X						X	X	X	X	X	X	X	X	X	X	X	X
IT	X	X	X		X	X		X	X		X	X	X	X					X	X	X	X	X

Figure 4.10 **The first and last activities will be eliminated because there are natural breaks in flow.**

With further scoping of the potential families completed, it's time to apply the 80 percent criteria. We will look for 80 percent similarity in the processing steps that are required to deliver the services (Figure 4.11).

	Submit Formal Request	Candidate Search	Contact Recruiter	Review Resume	First Interview	Evaluate Prior Research	Technical Test 1	Technical Test 2	Technical Test 3	Evaluate Test Results	Review First Interview Results	Second Interview	Review Second Interview Results	Vice President Interview	Review VP Interview Results	C-Suite Interview	Review C-Suite Interview Results	Final Interview	Review Final Interview Results	Configure Compensation Package	Create Offer Letter
Managers	X	X		X	X						X	X	X	X	X			X	X	X	X
Senior Execs.	X	X		X	X						X	X	X	X	X	X	X	X	X	X	X
Engineers	X	X		X	X		X			X	X	X	X					X	X	X	X
IT	X	X		X	X		X	X		X	X	X	X					X	X	X	X
R&D	X	X	X	X	X	X	X	X	X	X	X	X	X					X	X	X	X

Figure 4.11 **The matrix sorted with process similarity to reveal *potential* new hire service families.**

From Figure 4.11, it looks as though the business has three new hire service families:

1. Managers and Senior Executives

2. Engineers and IT

3. R&D

The next step in the process is to replace all the "Xs" with the time it takes to complete each activity as if only one person did it, then see if the variation in total work content time *within a potential family* exceeds 30 percent (Figure 4.12).

Helpful Hint

Once the team has determined the potential families, it's a good idea to give them a name or identity. This helps reinforce the message that the service family is defined by process steps and total work content. It also helps eliminate confusion with existing families that may have been developed for sales or other purposes.

	Submit Formal Request	Candidate Search	Contact Recruiter	Review Resume	First Interview	Evaluate Prior Research	Technical Test 1	Technical Test 2	Technical Test 3	Evaluate Test Results	Review First Interview Results	Second Interview	Review Second Interview Results	Vice President Interview	Review VP Interview Results	C-Suite Interview	Review C-Suite Interview Results	Final Interview	Review Final Interview Results	Configure Compensation Package	Create Offer Letter	Total Time
Managers	10	300		70	60						45	60	30	30	30			60	30	30	30	785
Senior Execs.	10	600		90	90						60	90	30	60	60	60	60	60	30	120	30	1450
Engineers	10	120		30	60		60			20	30	30	30					60	35	25	30	540
IT	10	120		25	60		60	60		40	30	30	30					60	35	25	30	595
R&D	10	900	900	60	90	60	90	90	90	90	60	30	45	30				30	30	60	30	2605

Figure 4.12 **The matrix with all the "Xs" replaced with process times in minutes.**

Applying the 30 percent criteria is important because while there might be enough similarity in process content to group services together into a family, the timing involved in completing all the activities required for each service may vary enough that the flow becomes choppy during the implementation, which is why this step is used to further refine the family. The formula used to determine the variation is:

(Highest – Lowest)/Highest

The R&D service family has only one service in it, and a review of the process times revealed no variation, so there is no need to perform this calculation.

The calculation for the potential Engineering and IT service family is:

595 min. – 540 min. = 55 min.

55 min./595 min. = 0.09, or 9%

Helpful Hint

To begin constructing a matrix for new hires, begin by looking at all the new hires that came through the business in the past 12 months or so. If the company is small and employees are not hired with great frequency, then it would be necessary to get a good sample size of what happened in the past year or two as a start.

The Engineering and IT service family is within the 30 percent guideline.

The calculation for the potential Managers and Senior Executives service family is:

1,450 min. – 785 min. = 665 min.

665 min./1,450 min. = 0.46, or 46%

There is too much variation in the total work content times of the services in this potential family. Therefore, the service family would be separated into two (Figure 4.13).

	Submit Formal Request	Candidate Search	Contact Recruiter	Review Resume	First Interview	Evaluate Prior Research	Technical Test 1	Technical Test 2	Technical Test 3	Evaluate Test Results	Review First Interview Results	Second Interview	Review Second Interview Results	Vice President Interview	Review VP Interview Results	C-Suite Interview	Review C-Suite Interview Results	Final Interview	Review Final Interview Results	Configure Compensation Package	Create Offer Letter	Total Time
Managers	10	300		70	60						45	60	30	30	30			60	30	30	30	785
Senior Executives	10	600		90	90						60	90	30	60	60	60	60	60	30	120	30	1450
Engineers	10	120		30	60		60			20	30	30	30					60	35	25	30	540
IT	10	120		25	60		60	60		40	30	30	30					60	35	25	30	595
R&D	10	900	900	60	90	60	90	90	90	90	60	30	45	30				30	30	60	30	2605

Figure 4.13 **The matrix divided into four new hire service families.**

Going forward, we will use the Engineering and IT service family. This family will require a current state map, the application of the nine guidelines, a designed future state, and an implementation plan. We will name this service family the *Technical New Hire* family. To implement value stream flow into the other three service families, the same methodology would be applied to each of them.

practical Engineering
application **Service Families**

Like most office departments, Engineering might have a great deal of variability in the process times of its activities due to the unpredictable nature of some of the work that flows in and out of this department. It may be possible to figure out a rough idea (particularly when it comes to any type of design work that needs to be done) of how long something will take in terms of its order of magnitude (minutes, hours, days, weeks, etc.), but it will often be difficult to pin down a precise time because most design work deals with unknown variables in one way or another.

As with the Human Resources example, the initial scope will focus on the functions in Engineering, which can then be expanded or collapsed as needed after the activities are determined. However, when we look at all the functions in Engineering, there can be a high variety of services that can be very complex, and creating the matrix could take weeks or longer if we encompass all of them.

Therefore, in our rough scope, along with natural breaks in flow and areas within our span of control, it's also important to consider which service we can transform within Engineering to make a working model of value stream flow that achieves Operational Excellence. Creating a working model is a great way to learn by doing, prior to taking on more complicated flows. For this reason, we would look for a service that happens repeatedly in our rough scope. In this case, we will choose Engineering Change Orders (ECOs), because this service will be a good working model to learn from before taking on more complex services in Engineering. If the scope of these services proves to be too small, it can always be expanded.

The service family matrix will be rough scoped for the many different types of ECOs that are provided. We again will look for 80 percent similar processing steps. Note that we have chosen "Receive Request" and "Upload to Operations DB" as the beginning and end of the service family (Figure 4.14).

	Receive Request	Log Request in Database	Preliminary Design	Log Preliminary Drawing	Materials Verification	Preliminary Design Review	Final Design	Final Design Review	FMEA	Log / Update Final Drawing	Cost Analysis	Certify Design	Eng. Manager Sign-Off	Finance Sign-Off	General Manager Sign-Off	Upload to Operations DB
Manufacturing Material Change	X	X			X		X	X	X	X	X	X	X	X	X	X
Customer Artwork Change	X				X		X	X		X	X	X	X	X		X
Customer Redesign	X	X	X	X	X	X	X	X	X	X	X	X	X	X	X	X
Application Design for Quote	X	X	X	X		X					X		X	X		
Yearly Product Update	X	X			X		X	X		X	X	X	X	X		X

Figure 4.14 **An initial matrix for the different types of ECOs.**

When the 80 percent analysis is run, it reveals the matrix seen in Figure 4.15.

	Receive Request	Log Request in Database	Preliminary Design	Log Preliminary Drawing	Materials Verification	Preliminary Design Review	Final Design	Final Design Review	FMEA	Log / Update Final Drawing	Cost Analysis	Certify Design	Eng. Manager Sign-Off	Finance Sign-Off	General Manager Sign-Off	Upload to Operations DB
Manufacturing Material Change	X	X			X		X	X	X	X	X	X	X	X	X	X
Customer Artwork Change	X				X		X	X		X	X	X	X	X		X
Yearly Product Update	X	X			X		X	X		X	X	X	X	X		X
Customer Redesign	X	X	X	X	X	X	X	X	X	X	X	X	X	X	X	X
Application Design for Quote	X	X	X	X		X					X		X	X		

Figure 4.15 **The matrix sorted to reveal potential service families.**

There are three families seen in Figure 4.15. While we could group the *Material Change, Artwork Change,* and *Yearly Update Change* services together, the *Customer Redesign* and *Application Design for Quote* families could not be grouped together due to the process flows being too different.

While having a family on its own may seem straightforward, it can be quite challenging. Therefore, we will select the *Customer Redesign* service family as our example.

With the 80 percent analysis complete, the next step would be to replace all the "Xs" with process times and see if the variation is less than 30 percent for the family. Since *Customer Redesign* is the only service *in* the family, it would appear that this step is not necessary. However, it's important to complete this step to see if there is variation in completing this single service based on other factors, such as the complexity of the preliminary design involved (modifying an off-the-shelf component vs. creating a design from scratch), the different tools used and knowledge needed, the application of the design, the environment in which the customer will use it, and many other factors.

In HR, the process times were predictable. In Engineering, the time it takes to come up with a design could have a wide range, so we will put these times into the matrix. We would not use average times, because this would be very misleading. We would always want to know roughly how long the easiest one takes and how long the more difficult ones take without factoring in strange anomalies that have occurred in the past (Figure 4.16).

	Receive Request	Log Request in Database	Preliminary Design	Log Preliminary Drawing	Materials Verification	Preliminary Design Review	Final Design	Final Design Review	FMEA	Log / Update Final Drawing	Cost Analysis	Certify Design	Eng. Manager Sign-Off	Finance Sign-Off	General Manager Sign-Off	Upload to Operations DB
Customer Redesign	10	10	15–240	20	20–60	30–200	0–120	0–120	60–120	10	30–90	60–90	5	5	5	15

Figure 4.16 **The matrix for the *Customer Redesign* service family, with each "X" replaced with a range of process times for each process.**

To further refine these ranges, we could look back at history for processes where the work content varies greatly. Here, these processes would be "Preliminary Design" and "Preliminary Design Review," and we'll examine the past 15 *Customer Redesigns* (Figure 4.17).

Completion Times at "Preliminary Design"		Completion Times at "Preliminary Design <u>Review</u>"	
"Customer Redesign" Number	Completion Time	"Customer Redesign" Number	Completion Time
1	13	1	25
2	17	2	30
3	60	3	60
4	240	4	190
5	55	5	55
6	220	6	180
7	15	7	35
8	70	8	73
9	14	9	33
10	260	10	200
11	60	11	56
12	250	12	170
13	19	13	28
14	50	14	61
15	255	15	165

Figure 4.17 **A dataset showing the process times for the "Preliminary Design" and "Preliminary Design Review" activities for the past 15 *Customer Redesigns*. Similar times have been color-coded.**

The times show that a relationship in the variation exists. Therefore, some factor is causing the times to extend. In this case, a talk with the engineers revealed it is the complexity of the design, so this factor will be used to further separate the *Customer Redesign* family into three separate families that should be grouped according to their complexity and total work content: *Standard, Moderate,* and *Complex Customer Redesigns* (Figure 4.18).

Helpful Hint

As with Human Resources, it is helpful to extend this analysis farther back in time. Make sure to get a good sampling of Customer Redesigns that have come into the business.

	Receive Request	Log Request in Database	Preliminary Design	Log Preliminary Drawing	Materials Verification	Preliminary Design Review	Final Design	Final Design Review	FMEA	Log / Update Final Drawing	Cost Analysis	Certify Design	Eng. Manager Sign-Off	Finance Sign-Off	General Manager Sign-Off	Upload to Operations DB	Total
Standard	10	10	15	20	20	30	n/a	n/a	60	10	30	60	5	5	5	15	295
Moderate	10	10	60	20	35	60	60	60	90	10	60	75	5	5	5	15	580
Complex	10	10	240	20	60	180	120	120	120	10	90	75	5	5	5	15	1085

Figure 4.18 **The service family matrix with all times filled in, showing the difference in work content between the *Standard, Moderate,* and *Complex Customer Redesign* families. Note that the *Standard* family does not require the "Final Design" or "Final Design Review" activities.**

With three families identified, we must decide which one to use for our first flow design and implementation. To make this decision, we would think about which ones will positively impact our customers and help us grow our business. In this case, the greatest number of ECOs tend to come through the *Moderate Customer Redesign* family, and the sales and marketing team has told us that our ability to smoothly and quickly make changes for customers is a feature that could really help them grow sales and market share. Additionally, the higher service level will help them maintain premium pricing. This makes the *Moderate Customer Redesign* family a good place to start, as a successful transformation will fuel business growth.

This family will require a current state map, the application of the nine guidelines, a designed future state, and an implementation plan. To implement value stream flow into the other two *Customer Redesign* service families, the same methodology would be applied to each of them.

Action Item

. . . .

Rough scope the potential areas in the office. Expand to natural breaks in flow. Determine service families for the selected scope. Following the methodology presented, select one service family to which the nine design guidelines for office flow will be applied.

Check off each step as it is completed.

☐ Rough scope the service families in the office, expanding or contracting the scope as necessary.

☐ Create a grid. Use the space provided on the following pages or a computer.

☐ List the services provided down the left-hand side.

☐ List the activities required to complete the services provided across the top.

☐ Place an "X" where an activity needs to be completed to provide a service.

☐ Refine the scope of the matrix if necessary. Look for natural breaks in flow and areas within your span of control as breaking points in the matrix.

☐ Group services based on an 80% similarity in activities required.

☐ Replace all "X's" with the time it takes to complete each activity as if only one person completed it.

☐ Determine if the variation in total work content time exceeds 30% within each potential service family.

☐ Based on the 80%, 30% guideline, adjust the service families (if necessary) by moving services to another family. Remember that it might not be possible to process the service in question anywhere else in the office.

☐ Select one service family to which the nine design guidelines for office flow will be applied. Remember that all of the design guidelines will have to be addressed, in order, for each service family created.

Acid Test

For the determined families, calculate the difference in the number of processing steps and the total work content. Compare these to the 80/30 guideline. Explain the potential for consistent flow while the demand for each service in the family could change each day.

Action Item
Determine Service Families

Activities Performed / Services Provided												

Describe the Service Family Chosen

Service family name

_____

_____

_____

Service provided

_____

_____

_____

Value stream starting point

_____

_____

_____

Value stream ending point

_____

_____

_____

Variation in total work content

_____

_____

_____

Notes

_____

_____

_____

chapter five

Create a Current State Value Stream Map for Each Service Family

After the service families have been scoped and selected, the next step is to create a current state map of how information flows and knowledge is captured in order to perform the service. It is important that when creating the current state map a team does it together by walking the office and asking questions of the people performing the work, such as:

- How do you know what to do next?

- Where do you get your work from?

- How long should it take you to perform your work?

- Where do you send your work once you are finished with it?

- How do you know when to send your work?

- What systems are required for this process?

- Is there a range of times required for the different types of work that come through this process?

- Do you ever have to clarify anything with other people via phone calls, emails, or some other means?

- Are you or other people available all the time to complete this work?

- How long does work typically wait before you can get to it?

- Is work delayed? If so, is it due to internal (within our company) or external (outside the company) reasons?

By performing this activity out in the office and not in a conference room with one or two people, the current state map becomes credible, which will be key when comparing it to the future state. A good map created in the office will show how work *actually* flows, as opposed to conference room versions that tend to show how work *should* flow.

Human Resources
Current State Map

After scoping the family based on process similarity and work content and identifying natural breaks in flow, the HR team would next create a current state map for the *Technical New Hire* service family (Figure 5.1). Note that the range of total process times is 515 to 620 minutes, not 540 to 595 minutes as seen in the service family matrix. This is because there is no set sequence in which the value stream processes candidates. The variation in total work content between 620 minutes and 515 minutes is only 17 percent, still well under the 30 percent guideline targeted.

Helpful Hint

A good current state map should show the following:

- How the service is initialized.

- All the processes involved in delivering the services. None should be omitted.

- How the processes are connected.

- How much inventory (emails, database backlog, or any other work) exists in between each process.

- Any wait time (internal) between the processes.

- Any delay time (external) between the processes.

- Any clarifications that happen between processes.

- Any management oversight or expedites that usually happen.

- The tools used at each process (local software, corporate systems, etc.).

- How knowledge is captured.

- Most importantly, the lead time ladder that depicts the service lead time compared to the amount of work time.

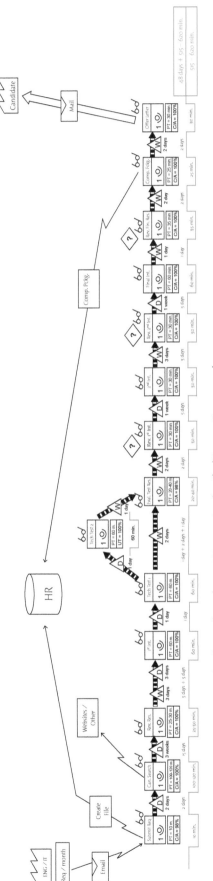

Figure 5.1 The current state map for the *Technical New Hire* service family (Human Resources).

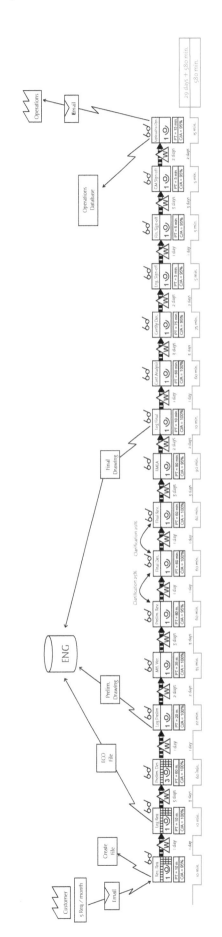

Figure 5.2 The current state map for the *Moderate Customer Redesign* service family (Engineering).

practical application   Engineering
Current State Map

With the family scoped according to process similarity and work content, and with natural breaks in flow identified, the Engineering team would create a current state map for the *Moderate Customer Redesign* service family (Figure 5.2).

Helpful Hint

We have provided a legend and glossary in the appendices to assist you if you are not familiar with value stream maps.

Action Item

· ·

Create a current state map showing the flow of information, inventory, waits, and delays, and a lead time ladder for the chosen service family.

Check off each step as it is completed.

☐ Create a current state map for the chosen service family.
   Use Appendix A for reference.

☐ Make sure to ask the questions listed on page 43.

☐ Make sure the current state map shows everything listed in the Acid Test.

Acid Test

· ·

Review the map created and check that the following items are present:

- How the service is initialized.

- All the processes involved in delivering the services.

- How the processes are connected.

- How much inventory (emails, database backlog, or any other work) exists in between each process.

- Any wait time (internal) between the processes.

- Any delay time (external) between the processes.

- Any clarifications that happen between processes.

- Any management oversight or expedites that usually happen.

- The tools used at each process (local software, corporate systems, etc.).

- How knowledge is captured.

- The lead time ladder that depicts the service lead time compared to the amount of work time.

Action Item
Draw the Current State Map

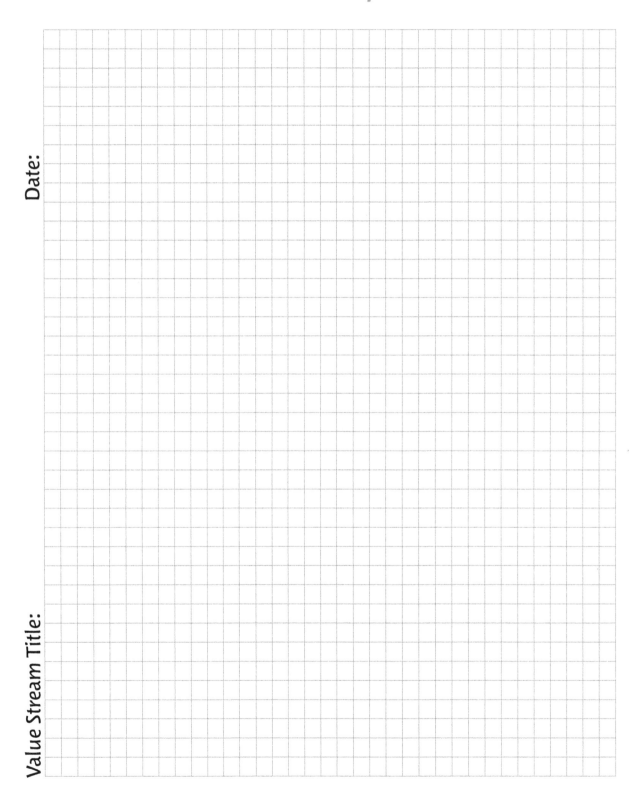

Date:

Value Stream Title:

part
two

Applying the Nine Guidelines
for Office Flow

chapter
six

Guideline #1: Takt and Takt Capability

Traditionally, takt time is defined as the rate of customer demand. In the office, it's often extremely difficult to determine true customer demand, or demand can be difficult to predict or highly erratic. It could be that the volume or the nature of requests that will come into the business tomorrow is impossible to predict, and this kind of wild variation has traditionally made applying Lean in the office challenging.

In order to handle high variation and erratic demand in an office environment, we will introduce a new concept called *takt capability*. Takt capability doesn't require us to know what the customer is going to request from us each day, but instead allows us to set multiple levels of ability to produce the service, and we then simply toggle between these levels.

Takt Capability

When high variation in demand is encountered, as is the case in most offices, the key is to use takt capability, which simply means setting a capability of what can be done in terms of mix and volume. For example, you may not know how many quote requests will be received each week, because this can be highly erratic. Therefore, you would set a takt capability of how many quotes could be completed in a week in terms of the volume of quotes *and* the mix of quotes.

The "volume" part of this description is easily understood, because it simply means *how many* quotes we can get done. However, the "mix" component may not be as clear. Mix refers to the different types of quotes in terms of the time they take to complete or the steps

For each service family:

Takt capability describes the designed output of the service in terms of volume and mix.

Takt time tells us how often work needs to be completed to meet the established takt capability.

through which they may go. For example, a *Quote Processing* service family may be made up of quotes that are relatively quick to complete (10 to 15 minutes), but also quotes that take longer to complete (2 to 3 hours).

Takt capability could be set at 20 quotes in a day (volume), which is easy to do if customers only request the quick quotes at 10 to 15 minutes each. However, if the mix changes and customers request 20 long quotes (2 to 3 hours), we can't meet the demand. Therefore, the takt capability refers to what combination or mix of "short" quotes and "long" quotes can be processed within a time period. An example of this would be: "Our takt capability is 20 quotes per day, with a maximum of 1 long quote per day."

There can certainly be a trade-off in the mix. As we add more long quotes to the mix, it will likely result in taking away some multiple of short quotes for each long quote added in order to stay within the takt capability. For example, every time we increase the capability to handle another long quote, it might mean taking away three short quotes in order to still be capable of processing all the work within the available time. In this case, we could state: "Our takt capability is 18 quotes per day, with a maximum of 2 long quotes per day." It's a good idea to really understand the potential demand for the service family in terms of volume before establishing takt capabilities. In order to do that, we would create a *demand profile*.

Demand Profiles

To determine the takt or takt capability, a demand profile must be created for the service family. A demand profile shows the total amount of work processed for all of the services provided by the family. Make sure to chart the demand information over a meaningful period of time. In a high-volume value stream, for example, three to six months worth of demand information may be sufficient, but be careful to think about the seasonality of sales or other factors that could cause significant volume changes. It's also possible to chart this forward into the future if you know what customers will be asking for in the near term.

Helpful Hint

When there is a lot of variation in demand, it's important to ask why. Is it external and the result of true customer demand (perhaps due to weather, which you cannot control), or is it internal and artificial demand (we only enter orders once per week)? The source of the variation needs to be investigated.

Having created the demand profile, step back and observe how much variation occurs. If the demand is smooth and without much variation, it may be possible to just set a takt time. If demand is erratic and/or you aren't able to predict it, draw a line that would satisfy customer demand 80 percent of the time. Using 80 percent as the target will allow the designed flow to handle 80 percent of the conditions that occur on a daily basis. Using a lower target like 50 percent would only allow the designed flow to handle 50 percent of conditions that occur on a daily basis. In Figure 6.1, a takt capability has been established that does this, represented by the horizontal line.

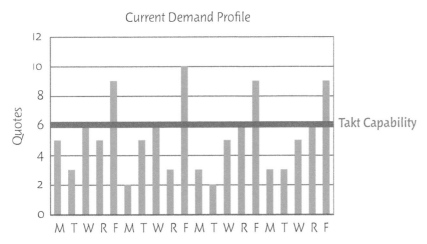

Figure 6.1 **A single takt capability capable of satisfying customer demand 80 percent of the time.**

Because demand can be erratic or unpredictable, having one takt capability for each service family might not be sufficient. In this case, the team might need to set up multiple takt capabilities that will enable the handling of different levels of customer demand. Practically speaking, different takt capability modes represent different ways of working. When demand changes, the team switches capability mode and the flow functions differently. Think of it like changing gears in a car. As the engine speeds up, the driver (or gear box) must eventually shift to a higher gear to handle the speed, otherwise the speed will be limited and eventually the engine will fail. The same thing happens in office flows if teams try to handle increases in demand without shifting gears.

Helpful Hint

If the service family selected has a work content range that is close to or exceeds the 30 percent guideline, we also should include an analysis of the mix showing how often the service with the highest work content occurs.

Figure 6.2 is the same demand graph, but now with multiple takt capabilities present: one mode that will satisfy demand 80 percent of the time, a second one for lower demand so the team isn't over-resourced in slower periods, and a third one for busy days when demand spikes.

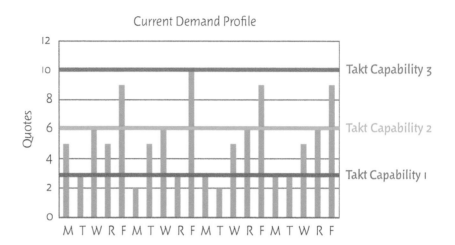

Figure 6.2 **The demand profile with three different takt capabilities.**

Calculating Takt Time

Takt capability is much more flexible than a typical takt calculation, which only considers volume and assumes each employee is available eight hours a day. Depending on the demand, the available time could be *chosen*, so we may have to decide how many hours employees are available to work on a particular service family. For each takt capability, the takt time equates to the available time divided by the demand. In the office, available time means for how long we will be able to allocate employees' time to work on a particular service family. Figure 6.3, for example, shows what the takt time would be for each takt capability for a given service family.

At this point in the design, we are only looking at the customer needs and the hours we want to spend delivering these needs. We haven't yet analyzed how long it takes to perform the service. This will happen in the next guideline.

Helpful Hint

Determining how many capability modes are required is a function of both the degree of variability in demand and the practicality of switching. In this case, three modes will be sufficient to allocate the correct resources and maintain flow while at the same time not causing the team to switch modes too often. If demand increases for longer than a day or two, there are several tools we can employ to handle it, which will be discussed in more detail in the final guideline.

In Figure 6.3, with the erratic demand that occurs for quoting, each takt capability would handle a certain number of quotes per day:

- Takt capability one: 3 quotes per day

- Takt capability two: 6 quotes per day

- Takt capability three: 10 quotes per day

For each takt capability, we would set a takt time, as seen in Figure 6.3. For takt capability one, we would like to set aside 30 minutes in the day for completing quotes. With a capability of 3 quotes per day, this means the takt time is 10 minutes.

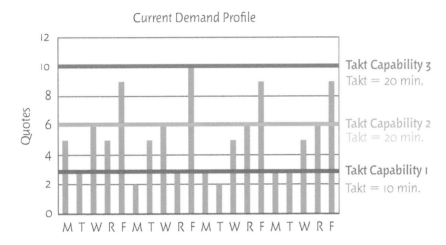

Figure 6.3 Each takt capability would have its own takt time, which would define the rate at which work would need to be completed to satisfy customer demand.

For takt capability two, we would like to set aside 120 minutes in the day for completing quotes. With a capability of 6 quotes per day, this means the takt time is 20 minutes.

For takt capability three, we would like to set aside 200 minutes in the day for completing quotes. With a capability of 10 quotes per day, this means the takt time is 20 minutes.

What this means is that normally the team will dedicate 120 minutes to processing quotes each day, because takt capability two will satisfy 80 percent of normal conditions. If the demand falls on a particular day, then the team will use takt capability one and spend only 30 minutes per day on quotes. If the demand spikes to 10 quotes per day, then the team will operate under takt capability three and spend 200 minutes per day on quotes.

In this manner, employees will have time available to fulfill the demand required for quoting, as well as enough time to spend on other tasks to meet the needs of the business and customers. As demand increases, more time is added to meet the higher demand, and we can always adjust the takt time up or down by adjusting the available time.

Human Resources
Takt and Takt Capability

In order to apply the first guideline to the *Technical New Hire* service family, we will have to determine if we can use a single takt time or if multiple takt capabilities will be required.

To determine this, we have created a demand profile for the past year that shows the demand for the service family (Figure 6.4).

Figure 6.4 shows there are some months when there aren't any *Technical New Hires* at all, while other months have a demand range of one to three per month.

Figure 6.4 **The demand profile for the *Technical New Hire* service family.**

As discussed earlier in this chapter, if a demand profile shows variation, then it's important to investigate why this is the case. After doing this, it was found that the variation has to do with where and when Human Resources searches for candidates in this service family. While Human Resources uses recruiters to search for personnel, the department also hires college and university graduates directly. This graduate hiring causes an influx of new hires in May when the candidates are finishing their studies.

This variation is outside of our control, so we will need to create takt capabilities that are able to handle the different volumes and mixes throughout the year. We would need to create one takt capability to handle demand for new hires 80 percent of the time. According to the demand profile, this takt capability will need to be able to handle one new hire per month (Figure 6.5).

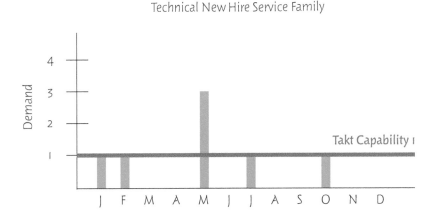

Figure 6.5 **The demand profile with a takt capability that satisfies demand 80 percent of the time.**

The takt capability set in Figure 6.5 is able to handle one new hire per month, either an engineer or an IT associate. In some months, there will be no new hires, meaning the flow for this service family will simply be inactive during those times and the processes not functioning or operating.

However, the takt capability created in Figure 6.5 will be unable to handle the spike in demand that is coming in May, or any other month where there is an unexpected spike in demand. To meet these increases in demand, a second takt capability will need to be created (Figure 6.6).

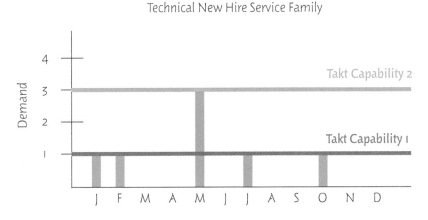

Figure 6.6 **The demand profile with a second takt capability created to handle the spike in demand that occurs in May.**

Going forward, the flow that is designed will need to be able to process candidates at the first takt capability level established, as the hiring of one new hire per month will satisfy customer demand 80 percent of the time.

The team will have to switch to takt capability mode two in May when the demand increases to three new hires during the college graduation season, or at any other time of year when they receive requests to hire more than one engineer or IT employee in one month.

Because hiring engineers and IT associates is so important to the business, we will allow the full eight hours in each day to serve as the available time. Therefore, determining the takt time for the established takt capability goes as follows:

Begin with the takt capability established to satisfy 80 percent of normal demand:

- 1 *Technical New Hire* per month

Define the available time:

- 1 month, or 160 hours (20 days x 8 hours per day)

Determine the takt time:

- Available Time ÷ Demand
- 160 hours ÷ 1 new hire = 160 hours

This means that over the course of a month, one technical new hire needs to be processed every 160 hours in order to keep up with demand. However, we need to understand how long we need to work on *Technical New Hires* each *day* in order to meet demand.

It takes roughly 10 hours to process one IT new hire (595 minutes), which is the longer of the two technical new hires. Because employees in the office are shared resources and they work on many different tasks throughout the day, we will spread out the 10 hours and allow a small amount of time each day (1/16th of a day) to be devoted to *Technical New Hires:*

- 1 day = 480 min. (8 hours x 60 min.)
- 480 min. x 1/16th (0.0625) = 30 min.

The amount of time *per day* that needs to be spent working on *Technical New Hires* is 30 minutes. This is the number that will be used in the next section on continuous flow to balance activities to takt time.

Figure 6.7 shows the current state map for the *Technical New Hire* service family with the takt time added in.

practical	Engineering
application	**Takt and Takt Capability**

To apply the first guideline to the *Moderate Customer Redesign* service family, we will have to determine if we can use a single takt time or if we will need to use multiple takt capabilities. Therefore, we have created a demand profile for the past year that shows the demand for this service family over the course of a year (Figure 6.8).

Figure 6.8 **The demand profile for *Moderate Customer Redesigns*.**

Due to the variation, which has been confirmed as externally generated and not within our control, multiple takt capabilities are needed to handle the differences in demand that appear month-to-month. In this case, there will be three different takt capability modes: one takt capability that can handle up to three *Moderate Customer Redesigns* a month, a second that can handle up to five, and a third that can handle up to seven (Figure 6.9).

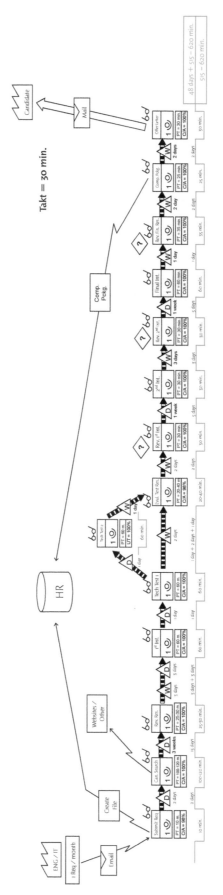

Figure 6.7 **The current state map for the *Technical New Hire* service family showing the takt time.**

Figure 6.9 **The three takt capabilities created for the *Moderate Customer Redesign* service family.**

The second takt capability handling up to five *Moderate Customer Redesigns* per month would satisfy customer demand 80 percent of the time and will be the mode the team uses most often, so this is the takt capability that will be used going forward when the rest of the design guidelines are applied to the service family. The team will shift up or down several times per year, but we will base the main design of flow on takt capability two, which will be the normal mode of operation.

Since *Moderate Customer Redesigns* fulfill such a critical business need and take priority, we will allow eight hours each day to serve as the available time. Therefore, determining the takt time for the established takt capability goes as follows:

Begin with the takt capability established to satisfy 80 percent of normal demand:

- 5 *Moderate Customer Redesigns* per month

Define the available time:

- 1 month, or 160 hours (20 days x 8 hours per day)

Determine the takt time:

- Available Time ÷ Demand
- 160 hours ÷ 5 Redesigns = 32 hours

This means that over the course of a month, one redesign needs to be completed every 32 hours in order to keep up with customer demand. However, we need to understand how long we need to work on *Moderate Customer Redesigns* each *day* in order to meet customer demand.

It takes roughly 10 hours to complete one *Moderate Customer Redesign* (580 minutes). Because employees in the office are shared resources and work on many different tasks throughout the day, we will spread out the 10 hours and allow a little less than one-third of each day (0.3 of a day) to be devoted to *Moderate Customer Redesigns:*

- 1 day = 480 min. (8 hours x 60 min.)

- 480 min. x 0.3 = 144 min.

The amount of time *per day* that needs to be spent working on *Moderate Customer Redesigns* is 140 minutes, rounded down from 144 minutes. This is the number that will be used in the next section on continuous flow to balance activities to takt time.

Figure 6.10 shows the current state map for *Moderate Customer Redesigns* with the takt time added in.

Helpful Hint

If you round takt times, be sure to round them down, not up, otherwise work will be completed at a slower pace than what is required to keep up with demand.

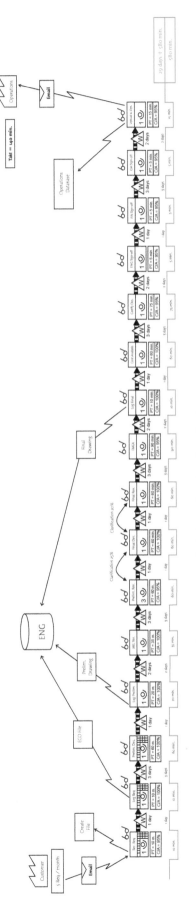

Figure 6.10 **The current state map for *Moderate Customer Redesigns* showing the takt time.**

Action Item

Create a takt time or takt capability for the service family chosen. Determine if variation in demand is truly generated by the customer or instead due to the way we process work internally.

Check off each step as it is completed.

☐ Create an *x* axis and *y* axis.

☐ Label the *x* axis with the length of time that makes sense for your business (e.g., days or months).

☐ Label the *y* axis with an amount or quantity interval that makes sense for your business (e.g., 10s or 20s).

☐ Label the graph with the name of the service family chosen.

☐ Research and graph the demand profile for the service family chosen.

☐ Determine a takt capability for the service family that will satisfy customer demand 80 percent of the time.

☐ Determine a takt time for the established takt capability.

☐ If applicable, determine how many takt capabilities are needed and at what level they will need to be.

☐ Determine the takt time for each additional takt capability created.

Acid Test

Check to see if a person not familiar with the service can understand the takt or takt capability being used. Can they determine the output ability for the family?

Action Item
Create a Demand Profile

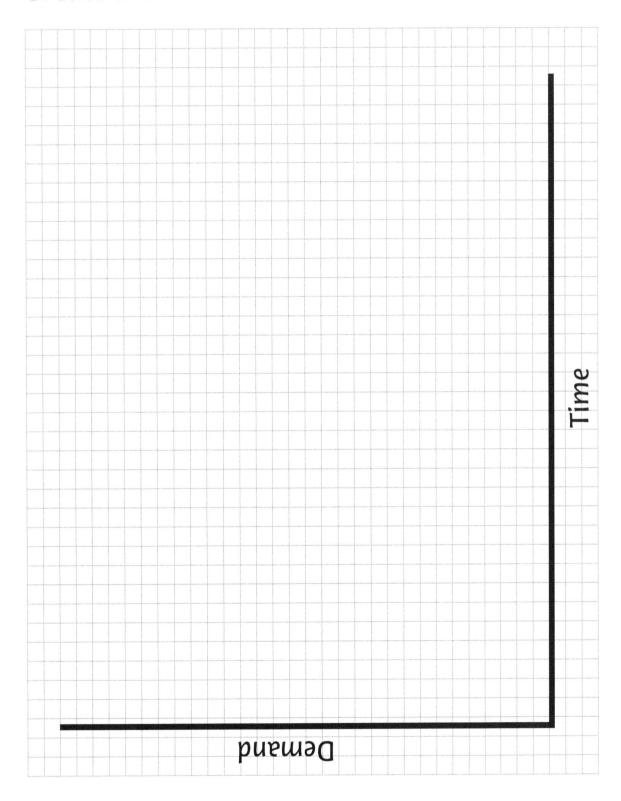

Describe the Takt Capability Created

Number of takt capabilities

_____

_____

_____

Demand each takt capability will handle

_____

_____

_____

Available time for each takt capability

_____

_____

_____

Takt time established for each takt capability

_____

_____

_____

Frequency with which we will switch takt capability modes

_____

_____

_____

Notes

_____

_____

_____

chapter seven

Guideline #2: Continuous Flow

In the office, continuous flow means completing one activity and moving the work on to the next process in the flow, without stoppage or interruption. Try to think of this as working in a *process one, move one* fashion.

A Typical Office

Traditionally, work is completed in the office using what might be called the "self-prioritization" method, where individual tasks or pieces of work are completed by an employee according to his/her own personal method of prioritization (Figure 7.1). Each employee might have a different way of answering the question: "How do I know what to work on next?"

Once work has been completed, it is normally "pushed" to the next process in the flow *regardless of whether the next process needs it* (Figure 7.2).

Work moves from one person or process to another, where it usually sits and waits to be completed along with many other jobs. It's generally hard to know how long work will remain in someone's inbox before it is processed because each job competes with every other job for the employee's time and is subject to each individual's method of prioritization. In this situation, the delivery time to the customer is highly variable and unrelated to any other job. This usually results in team members or managers prioritizing and expediting to meet customer deadlines (or often

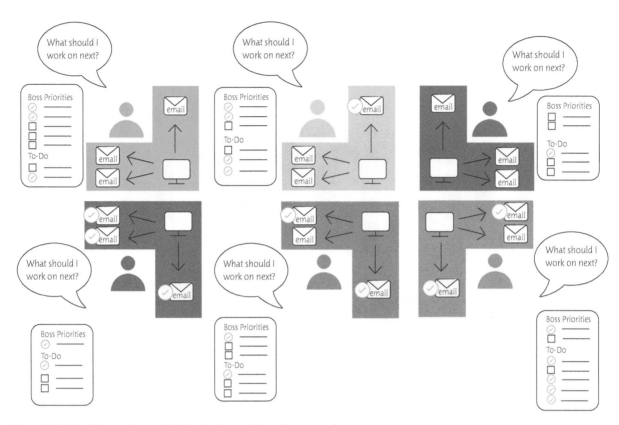

Figure 7.1 Typically, employees decide for themselves what to work on next.

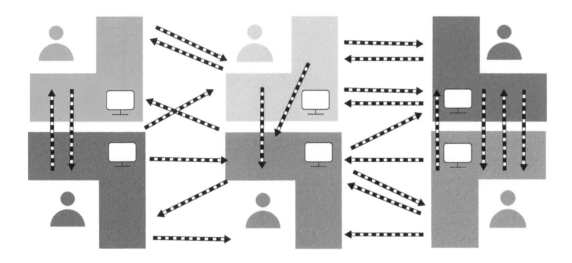

Figure 7.2 Work, which could be physical or electronic, is pushed from process to process in the office, regardless of whether it is ready to be received and worked on.

investing time renegotiating deadlines). With so much high variation in workflow and unpredictable customer demand, teams end up holding regular status meetings to reestablish priorities and shuffle work.

Part-Time Continuous Flow

In order to mitigate or eliminate the variation that occurs between processes, and to consistently deliver information to the customer, it would be great if we could put a physical conveyor that connects all the processes and moves information at the speed the customer wants (Figure 7.3). This would create full-time continuous flow throughout the office.

Definition

Continuous flow
means working in a process one, move one fashion.

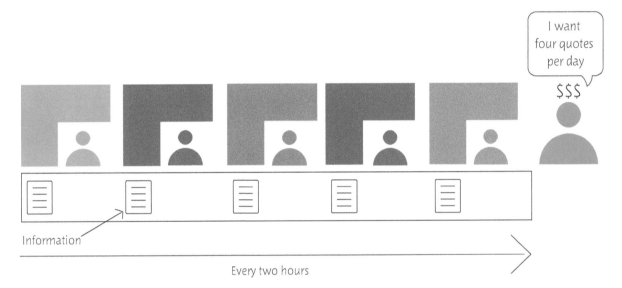

Figure 7.3 **A conveyor belt moving work in continuous flow at a preset rate to the customer to satisfy demand.**

However, we cannot turn the office into an assembly line. Could we drop the physical conveyor and simply locate desks next to each other 100 percent of the time and process work in a dedicated flow fashion? Perhaps, if the demand each day warranted. In most offices, however, employees are tasked with many different responsibilities and are shared among many different services. It is usually not possible to dedicate employees 100 percent of the time to a single service family on a full-time basis. Therefore, when we cannot dedicate people fully to a single service family, the next best thing is to create part-time *processing cells* that meet at preset times throughout the day or week.

Definition

. . . .

Processing cells are
areas of the value
stream where work is
completed in continuous flow.

The employees in these cells would meet and flow work in a continuous
flow fashion for only a certain amount of time, then go back to their other
responsibilities. They would have all of the tools and equipment needed in
the processing cell when and where it meets so all of the work could be
completed before being moved to the next activity in the flow (Figure 7.4).

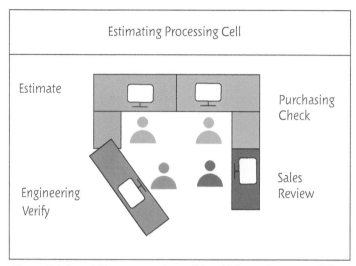

Figure 7.4 **A part-time processing cell in which employees work in a
process one, move one fashion.**

It's important to note that Figure 7.4 shows a part-time processing cell for
one service family, not the entire matrix. Each part-time processing cell
created in the flow will complete work for one service family, and there
might be multiple cells within one entire end-to-end flow. Additionally,
while it would be great if all the activities in the service family could be
placed into continuous flow via processing cells, it is often unrealistic or
simply not possible to do this. In these situations, creating processing cells
wherever possible will still yield benefits.

A great example of a practical application of a processing cell is for approvals.
Consider a situation where multiple people need to sign off on a request, such
as a capital expenditure request. These kinds of sign-off chains are normally
lengthy and unpredictable. A processing cell can be created to gather all the

Helpful Hint

. . . .

In office flows, wait times are often the biggest problem. A piece of work, such as an approval request, might be sent
to a manager in a timely fashion, but end up sitting in his inbox until he gets to it, whenever that may be. The power of
reducing or removing waits is not to be underestimated and is one of the benefits of creating processing cells.

managers responsible for signing off on capital expenditure requests together in the same room, perhaps once a week. This "signing party" would take all the week's CAPEX (capital expenditure) requests and sign off on them in a process one, move one fashion. Once a request enters the processing cell, it would get all the signatures required (or be rejected) with no wait time between each manager. This would allow approvals to happen predictably, and everyone would know exactly when they would take place.

Processing cells can even be created when employees are not present in the same building. Virtual or home office work cells can be established using email rules that funnel work by service family into the proper subfolder. Then, at a preestablished time, an employee would process work from that folder and email it to the next person in the flow, who would then process it. This would continue until all work was completed, thus preserving the principle of process one, move one.

Obstacles to Continuous Flow

Creating processing cells can be challenging. Below are some common obstacles that may be encountered when trying to create continuous flow, and some thoughts on how to mitigate them. Keep this list handy when working with a team when identifying opportunities to create continuous flow processing cells:

Obstacle – Cultural: Employees may not be accustomed to working in continuous flow or do not want to relinquish a personalized workspace, or they are just worried they will get bored.

Solution: The part-time dedicated flow idea resolves these issues, because employees may only be required to participate in continuous flow once a day, once a week, or whatever the value stream requires, but it will never be their entire role.

Obstacle – Geographical: Employees do not physically work near one another or are located in different buildings (or states or countries).

Solution: While full-time continuous flow may require a business to reconfigure the layout of its office, using part-time dedicated cells means that participants can simply gather in a booked meeting room, office, breakroom, kitchen, or even a local café to perform the work for a portion of each day or week. It's even possible to create virtual work cells, where work is completed at one location then emailed or uploaded into a database and completed in another location using the same principles of *process one, move one*. While virtual cells are certainly a possibility, try creating a physical processing cell in one site first to try out the idea of continuous flow.

Obstacle – Digital: These days, much of the work people move around their offices is digital, which generally means figuring out how to make flow visual even when it is buried in someone's computer.

Solution: If a co-located team is moving work between themselves but via email or some other digital means, then think about making the flow visual. A good tip is to consider how you can make the digital into the physical. For example, some companies have a system where a baton is passed between members of a processing cell as the work moves around it. Even though the actual work is hidden in someone's computer, anyone walking by can see where the work is by looking for the baton, a great visual signal.

Virtual work cells also can help deal with the digital realities of the modern office. The same techniques for creating continuous flow can still be used in a primarily digital environment when people may not have the option of co-locating; we may just have to modify them. The processing cell might never physically come together, but would instead occur at preset times throughout the day as certain employees all use their electronic resources at the same time to process work for one particular service family. The employee who occupies the first position in this virtual processing cell could then email his or her work to the next employee in the virtual processing cell, and so on down the line. The key is having the commitment to the processing cell; if an employee is part of a virtual processing cell, they must begin working on the next piece of work in the flow the minute it arrives in their inbox. It's important that employees block time in their calendars to be available to do the work in a process one, move one fashion. They can't be in a meeting or on the phone when they are needed by the virtual cell. They must be dedicated to the processing cell at the right time.

Obstacle – Unsuitable Processes: This could be creatively oriented process-es (e.g., creative design) in which creating continuous flow is challenging to implement. Sometimes, it doesn't make sense to break up a process among different employees, because it may cause more issues than it resolves. You would probably not want one graphic designer creating one half of a print advertisement and another picking it up to complete the other half. It's unlikely they would match.

Solution: Even with flows that involve a lot of creativity, it may still be possible to create a processing cell for the processes that come before or after the ones that are creatively oriented, or even for *parts* or *sections* of the creatively oriented process, which then would allow the team to realize some of the benefits of working in continuous flow.

Obstacle - Multiple Responsibilities: Employees have many different things they need to work on each day, and cannot be dedicated in a way that supports continuous flow.

Solution: Remember that part-time processing cells are created in the office precisely because of this fact. Employees will still be able to spend time completing other work and fulfilling their other responsibilities during the day, outside of the time set aside for continuous flow processing.

Creating Processing Cells

The first step in creating processing cells is to balance the work to customer demand, or takt time. Start by reviewing the selected service family and deciding where to combine activities and move them one at a time at the rate of customer demand. A *balance chart* is the perfect tool for figuring out where these opportunities exist. It depicts the activities needed, the people who currently perform them, and the takt time for the activities.

The analysis required to develop a processing cell is as follows: Start by creating a rough balance chart showing all the processes, then move on to analyze in greater detail any processes that seem like good candidates for processing cells using *stack graphs*. Then, having rebalanced the target processes to takt, you can create the final balance chart showing the finalized times.

Figure 7.5 shows what the first step would look like where we create a rough balance chart.

With the balance chart laid out, the next step is to look for opportunities for continuous flow. Start by looking at processes with similar times that are next to each other. In Figure 7.5, the circled processes all have process times relatively close to one another and may represent an opportunity for continuous flow, while none of the other processes have this potential.

Definition

···

A **work element** is
defined as the small-
est amount of work
that could be moved to and
completed by another person.

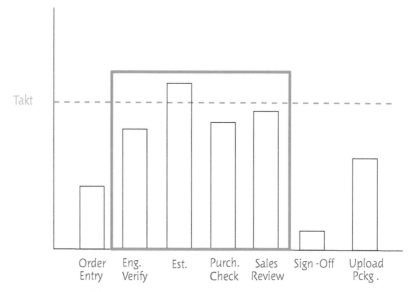

Figure 7.5 **A rough balance chart showing the process time of each activity in the service family.**

Once these opportunities have been identified, it's time to dig deeper and determine exactly how work could flow through the cell. We isolate each process and show the core and noncore work that needs to be done at each one. In addition to this, we also show all of the *work elements* involved in completing the activity and how long each one takes (Figure 7.6).

Core work describes activities that must be completed by a specialist, and this is work that normally requires some sort of detailed training or experience in the respective field to complete. Noncore work describes work that can be completed by someone else in the cell with very little training, meaning it could be moved around or perhaps even eliminated if it is non-value added. Any activity currently being completed but that could be eliminated without affecting the delivery of the service would be considered waste and should be eliminated.

An example of core work versus noncore work would be the design work done by an engineer. The actual activity of creating a design would be considered core work, because no one else would be able to do it without significant training or experience in the field. Entering the design specifications into a database or setting up a project in the company's project management software, on the other hand, could be considered noncore work because non-engineers could be taught how to complete these tasks with some cross-training.

Creating a detailed stack graph showing core and noncore work allows us to balance the work to takt time by moving around noncore work elements. To do this, we create a detailed stack graph for each process and identify all

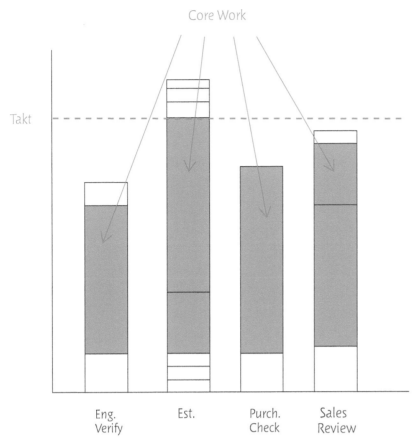

Figure 7.6 **A stack graph for the processes identified for a continuous flow processing cell.**

the work elements that need to be completed. Doing this then reveals which ones can be moved to another process in order to balance to takt. We also can balance by looking for activities that just don't need to be done, or waste. Removing these activities can help balance to meet takt time. Figure 7.7 shows the detailed stack graph for the "Estimate" process.

From Figure 7.7, it's clear that certain noncore work elements don't have to be processed by the estimator and could be done by other employees.

Figure 7.8 shows the "Estimate" stack graph with the first three and last three noncore work elements removed. The first three noncore work elements, "Fill out header information," "Enter header information into database," and "Enter customer information into database," would be moved to the "Eng. Verify" process. The last three noncore work elements would be moved to the "Purch. Check" process.

If it's not possible to balance all the processes precisely to takt and some are lower than the takt time, employees could bring other work to the processing cell and complete it while they are waiting to continue the work

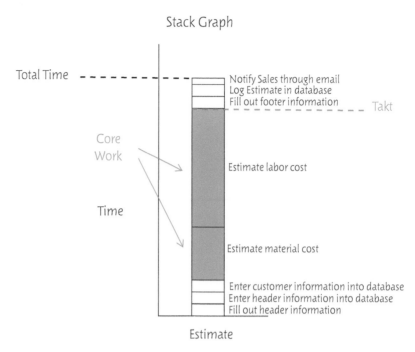

Figure 7.7 **A stack graph for the "Estimate" process.**

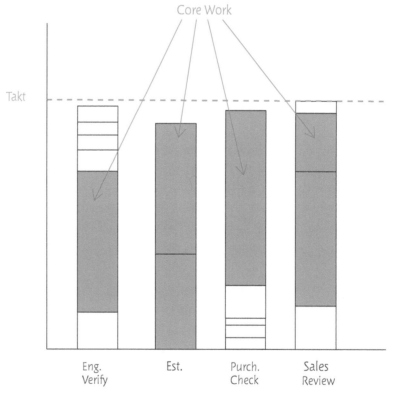

Figure 7.8 **The new balance chart with work elements rebalanced to takt.**

of the processing cell. The work of the processing cell must always take priority, however, so care needs to be taken when determining what this "other" work should be, because the more involved or demanding it is, the more likely it will be to interfere with the work of the processing cell.

The Physical Layout

Once the processing cell has been created using balance charts, it's time to begin laying out what the processing cell would physically look like and how it would actually operate. This would include the number of workstations needed, what equipment or software is needed, where the work would be located between stations, where the inputs and outputs of the processing cell would be, and at what time or times the processing cell would meet on a regular basis.

The physical layout should include:

- Network connections.

- Access to shared drives.

- Printers.

- Computer workstations or a set place for laptops.

- Exterior monitors for laptops to make the screen size comfortable and comparable to what employees have at their full-time workstations.

- Correct furniture.

- Reference material in the room.

Helpful Hint

It's important that when the processing cell comes together that all members be present. If there are any questions, then the other people in the processing cell would be available to answer them. If a person cannot attend the processing cell, they should send a designated representative.

practical **Human Resources**
application **Continuous Flow**

The takt capability established tells us we need to be able to hire one engineer or IT associate per month. Back in the section on takt capability, we determined that the takt time is 30 minutes.

Now that a takt time has been established that can be used for balancing processes for continuous flow, we need to look at the balance chart for all of the activities required to deliver this service. In Figure 7.9, a line has been overlaid showing the takt that will be used for balancing.

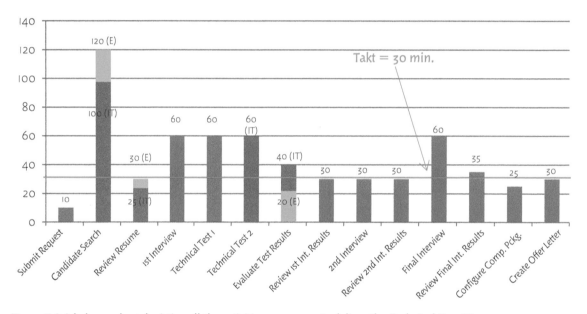

Technical New Hire Balance Chart

Figure 7.9 A balance chart depicting all the activities necessary to deliver the *Technical New Hire* service family. Blue bars indicate common tasks, orange is specific to engineering candidates, and purple is specific to IT candidates.

Most of the activities have the same process time regardless of whether an engineering or IT candidate is up for consideration. However, there are exceptions. IT candidates must pass through a second technical test activity, while the engineering candidates only need to take one technical test. Additionally, at some of the activities, it takes longer to process the engineering candidates than it does to process the IT candidates, or vice versa.

The goal is to create continuous flow processing cells wherever possible. Therefore, we will look to where neighboring processes have similar process times. The first three processes won't work because there is high variation in the process times between them.

Figure 7.10 shows the potential areas of continuous flow that would be worth looking into.

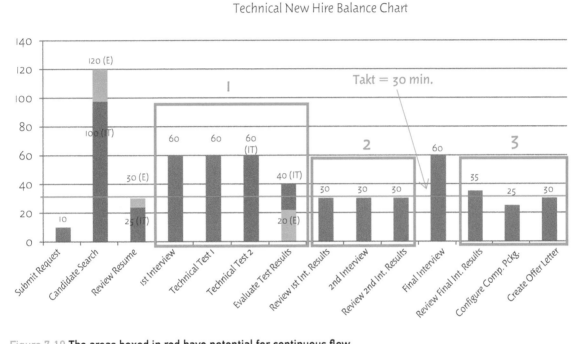

Figure 7.10 **The areas boxed in red have potential for continuous flow.**

It won't be possible to balance the first group of activities to the established takt time, but it's still possible to process candidates in a "process one, move one" fashion. As soon as a candidate is finished with the first interview, he or she would proceed immediately to the first technical test, and then to the second technical test in the case of an IT candidate (engineering candidates would simply go home at this point).

Although the process times would not be balanced to takt, processing candidates in this way (or processing the work involved with them) would still yield benefits to the organization in the form of less waiting between activities, less reprioritization, etc., so continuous flow would be targeted here with this first grouping. This processing cell will be called the *First Interview Processing Cell.*

While the second grouping of processes have similar process times, it would actually be very difficult to implement continuous flow. Once the "Review First Interview Results" activity has been completed, there is a natural break in flow, as the candidates will leave while the interview results are discussed and the second interviews are scheduled.

The third grouping is a good candidate for creating a processing cell, as the process times are close together and the candidates do not need to be present. Stack graphs need to be developed to see if this would be possible (Figure 7.11).

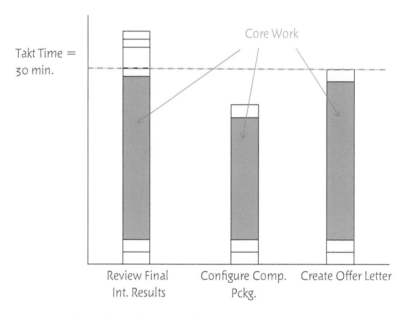

Figure 7.11 **The stack graphs for the final three activities in the flow.**

From the stack graphs seen in Figure 7.11, the final activity is balanced right to takt while the others are either above or below. At "Review Final Int. Results," the final work elements involve clerical work like logging the selected candidate's data into different systems, so this is work that could be transferred to the "Configure Comp. Pckg." process in order to balance them to takt (Figure 7.12). This processing cell would be called the *Offer Letter Processing Cell.*

In terms of constructing the physical layout for this processing cell, it may be possible to create simply by arranging the people around a conference room table if the work is portable enough to be completed with laptops. The physical layout is something to work out in detail when implementing the design, but whatever is determined, it's crucial to ensure that the part-time processing cell has all the equipment, space, and materials it

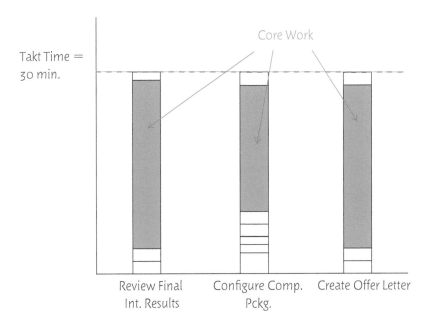

Figure 7.12 **The stack graphs balanced to takt.**

needs to ensure the seamless flow of work from process to process, as well as anything else that would be needed to make sure there are no interruptions in the flow. Figure 7.13 shows a mock-up of the processing cell or workspace layout.

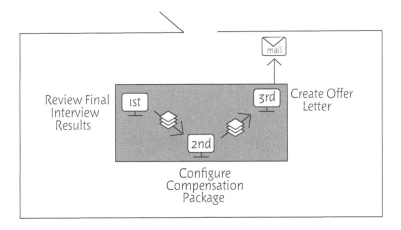

Figure 7.13 **Here is what the setup of the processing cell could look like, with the required employees seated around a conference room table and flowing work in a process one, move one fashion.**

Figure 7.14 shows the final balance chart with both processing cells identified.

Technical New Hire Balance Chart

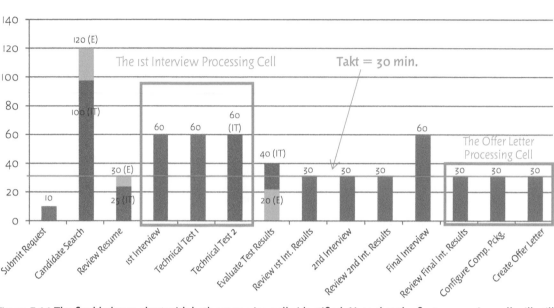

Figure 7.14 **The final balance chart with both processing cells identified. Note that the first processing cell will still work in a process one, move one fashion even though it is not balanced to takt time.**

Figure 7.15 shows what the value stream map would look like with the processing cells created.

Engineering
Continuous Flow

Most of the engineers and other employees that process the three types of *Customer Redesigns* are shared resources, and they will have other service families to work on as well, so creating full-time processing cells for the *Moderate Customer Redesign* service family will be very difficult. Therefore, we will try to create part-time processing cells where possible.

The takt capability established tells us we need to be able to be able to process five *Moderate Customer Redesigns* per month, and we determined that the takt time necessary to achieve this is 140 minutes. Therefore, each process needs to allow 140 minutes per day to process work for this service family.

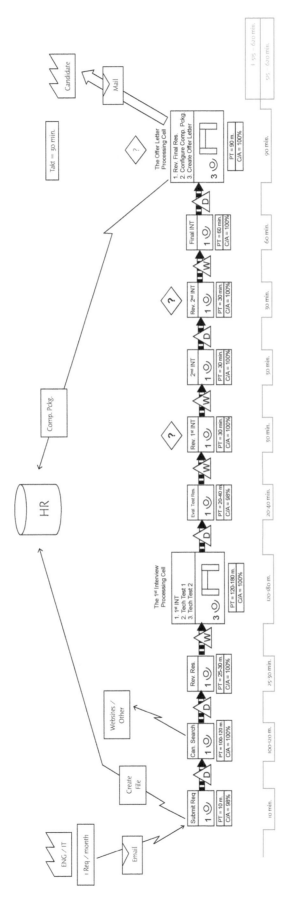

Figure 7.15 The value stream map for the *Technical New Hire* service family with the two processing cells created.

Figure 7.16 shows the balance chart for all the activities required to deliver the *Moderate Customer Redesign* service.

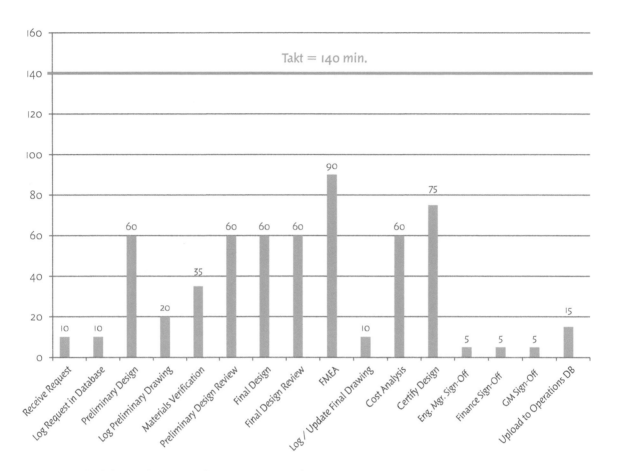

Figure 7.16 **The balance chart for *Moderate Customer Redesigns.***

Before going on to explore the options that exist for creating processing cells, some attention needs to be given to the "Preliminary Design" process, because it is unique. Recall that a range of process times exists at this process depending on whether the *Customer Redesign* falls into the *Standard*, *Moderate*, or *Complex* family. Additionally, before the work of "Preliminary Design" is completed, it will be difficult to know in which family a *Customer Redesign* belongs.

Perhaps a senior engineer would be able to determine this after just the first two processes in the flow, but it's more likely the business will have no way of reliably knowing what type of *Customer Redesign* it is dealing with until some design-oriented work has been completed, and the first place where this will happen is "Preliminary Design."

Because of this, it might be very difficult to put "Preliminary Design" into *any* processing cell. If there is no way of knowing how long a particular *Customer Redesign* will take at "Preliminary Design" until at least some work has been completed on it, then there will be no way of knowing whether the takt time for a given family has been exceeded until it is too late.

With the takt time so high, and with "Preliminary Design" eliminated from continuous flow consideration, it would appear as though continuous flow could potentially be created wherever the process times of more than one process could be added up close to takt. In Figure 7.17, we can see that this could happen virtually anywhere.

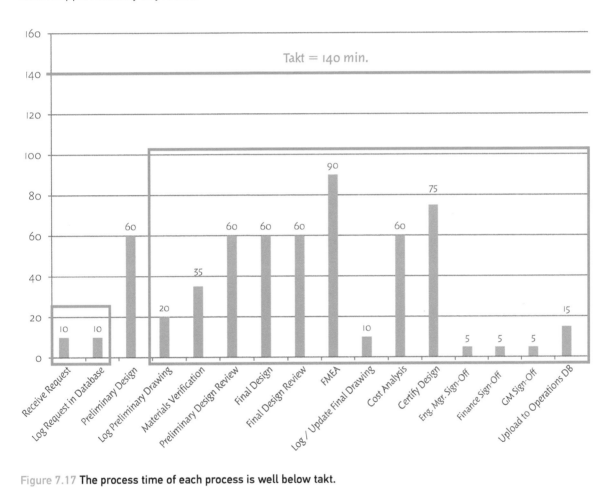

Figure 7.17 **The process time of each process is well below takt.**

This situation presents some additional opportunities, as we can look to combine processes and still be under takt time. For example, the first two processes, "Receive Request" and "Log Request in Database," can be combined into a singular process. This same thinking can be applied to the "Log/Update Final Drawing" and "Cost Analysis" processes (Figure 7.18).

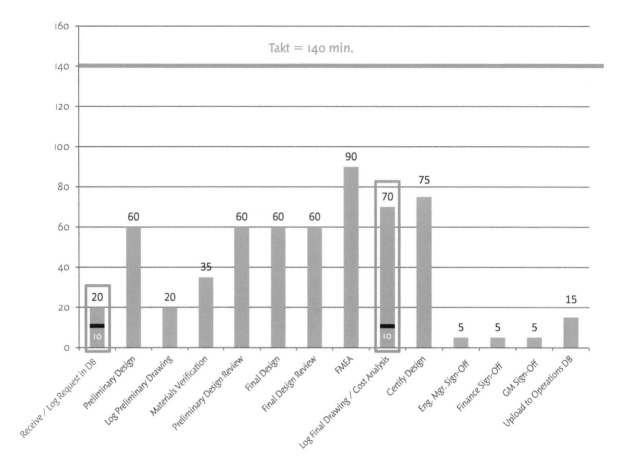

Figure 7.18 **In two separate places, two processes have been combined into one (the red boxes). The horizontal line shows where the time for the first part of the job will end.**

Combining processes can be very beneficial. When processes are combined, it removes an opportunity for information to stagnate and wait or be reworked once the second process receives it. The biggest benefit when we combine processes is that it will help us know consistently when the work will be completed, as we have eliminated the waits, delays, errors, and more that happen between separated processes, which is a good thing.

For the remaining processes, however, this strategy simply won't work, because they require too much experience or training or involve employees who may have some specific skills that are in such high demand that their time shouldn't be spent on simpler clerical work. In certain cases it would create situations where one employee would end up reviewing his own work, which would be undesirable.

The following groups of processes can be put together into continuous flow processing cells (Figure 7.19). Between these groupings, there are conditions that prohibit adding more processes to the processing cell.

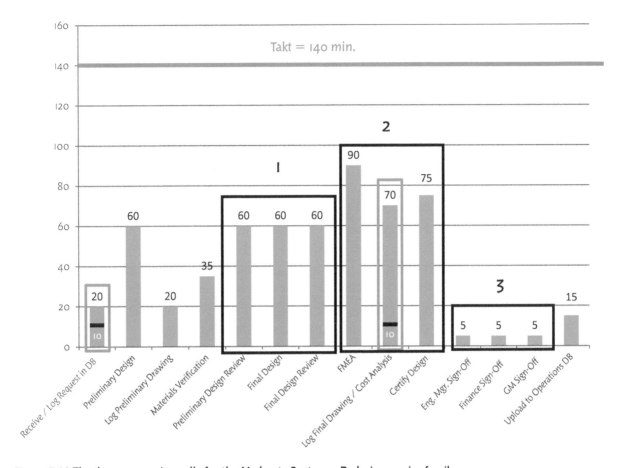

Figure 7.19 **The three processing cells for the *Moderate Customer Redesign* service family.**

The first group of processes we might put into a processing cell are "Preliminary Design Review," "Final Design," and "Final Design Review." From a purely mathematical perspective, creating a processing cell would not be an issue, because each process is well under takt. It is not possible to combine any processes together, however. The three processes would maintain their original process times and be placed into a processing cell called the *Design Review Processing Cell.* Here, they would complete work in a process one, move one fashion. Having all three employees in the same room together means they have an opportunity to ask questions and clarify design issues on the spot. The employees at the second and third positions could simply bring other work to complete until their work begins in the processing cell.

Co-locating in this manner also means that almost *all* the design and review work happens in the same place and at the same time, with only the design work at "Preliminary Design" happening outside the cell. There would be no more tracking down a senior person for reviews, sending them emails, or making phone calls to inquire whether or not a *Moderate Customer Redesign* has been reviewed. It would simply happen by the end of this processing cell, a tremendous benefit to the organization.

For the second set of processes, a processing cell could still be created even though all the process times are under takt. This processing cell will be called the *Analyze and Certify Processing Cell*. Because the processing cell will only meet part-time, there is no danger of completing more work or completing it faster than the customer wants it. If no *Moderate Customer Redesigns* have come into the business, then the value stream, and this processing cell, would simply be inactive. Arranging the processes in a process one, move one fashion eliminates the handoffs that would otherwise bog down the flow.

The third group of processes also could be combined into a processing cell, called the *Sign-Off Processing Cell*. In addition to the typical benefits of co-location, creating a processing cell would ensure these senior employees make time in their busy schedules specifically dedicated to the *Moderate Customer Redesign* flow. There would be no more worrying or wondering when the engineering manager (for example) would sign off on a *Moderate Customer Redesign*. It would simply happen by the end of the processing cell, meaning *Moderate Customer Redesigns* will always be signed at the same time each day or week; no need to chase any signatures (Figure 7.20).

The total number of handoffs in the value stream has been significantly reduced, which will eliminate opportunities for work to stop and accumulate or become reprioritized. This reduces the overall lead time through the flow by eliminating waiting.

Furthermore, *no additional work has been added to this value stream*. This can be an important point to emphasize as teams begin to implement the concepts. Knowing that the total process time remains the same, the team can be confident that the flow being designed is simply a better way of operating, not one that involves more work for them.

Figure 7.21 shows what the value stream map would look like with the processing cells created. Note that the clarification loops that were present previously are gone, as any clarification needed now takes place within the processing cell when it meets. While reduced, clarifications will still happen, but there will now be no time spent waiting for an answer.

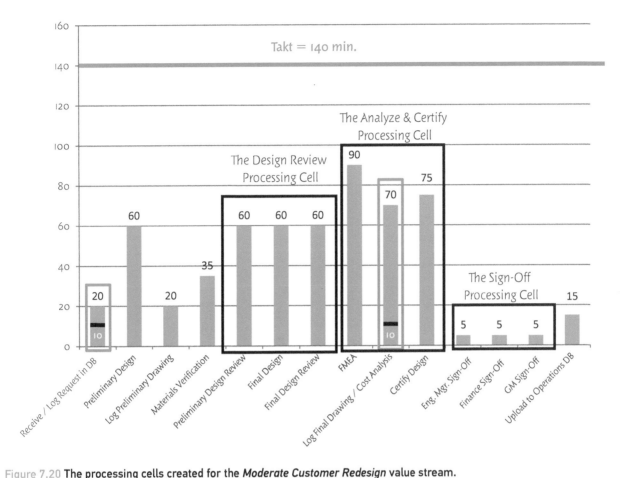

Figure 7.20 **The processing cells created for the *Moderate Customer Redesign* value stream.**

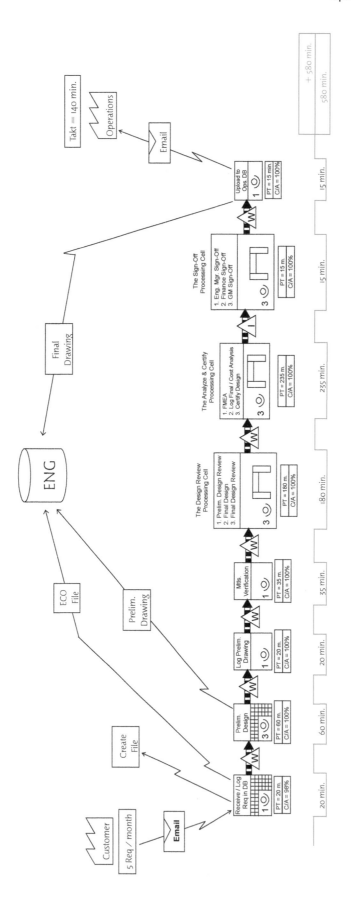

Figure 7.21 **The value stream map for *Moderate Customer Redesigns* with the three processing cells created.**

Action Item

Where possible, create part-time processing cells for the service family chosen.

Check off each step as it is completed.

☐ Create a rough balance chart showing the process times of all the processes in the service family compared to takt.

☐ Identify opportunities for continuous flow processing cells by looking at where the process times of neighboring processes are close to takt.

☐ Create stack graphs for each process and shift around work elements as needed to balance to takt.

☐ Determine which employees and which skill sets are needed to complete the work in the processing cell.

☐ Create a new balance chart showing which processes will be combined into processing cells.

☐ Determine what equipment, materials, network connections, employees, skill sets, and so on are needed to complete the work in the processing cell.

☐ Draw a mock-up of the physical layout of the processing cell. Be sure to label which processes are there.

Acid Test

Check to ensure work is being performed in a process one, move one fashion without interruption.

Action Item
Create Continuous Flow Processing Cells

1. Input the takt time where shown.

2. List the process times for each process in the service family as bar graphs along the *x* axis.

3. Identify where the process times of neighboring processes are close to takt.

4. Try to balance processes for continuous flow by shifting work elements.

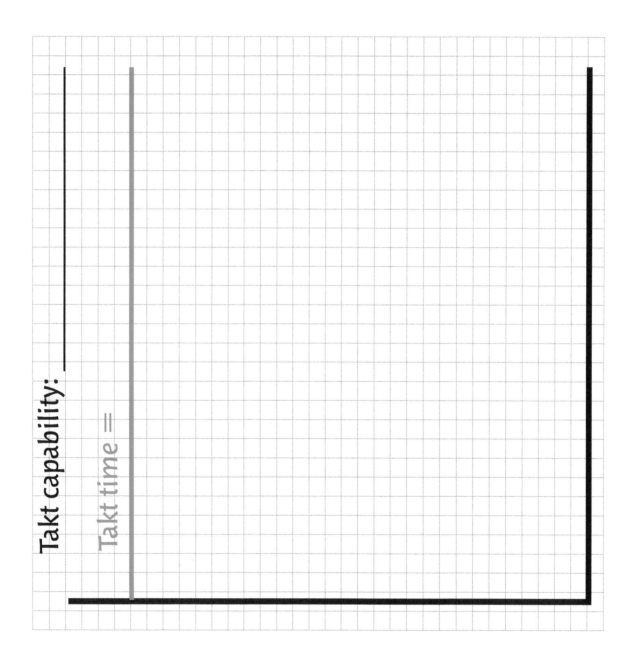

Describe the Processing Cell Created

Time the processing cell will happen

_____

_____

_____

Location of the processing cell

_____

_____

_____

Employees who will be involved

_____

_____

_____

Skill sets required

_____

_____

_____

Work that will be completed

_____

_____

_____

Process time for each employee

_____

_____

_____

Notes

_____

_____

_____

chapter
eight

Guideline #3: FIFO

With opportunities identified for creating continuous flow processing cells, the next step is to connect these cells and other processes in flow. Where processes can't be combined or put into continuous flow, they should be connected using FIFO (first in, first out).

FIFO is still a form of flow, because work is moving forward in sequence without priority changes, reroutes, or management decisions. FIFO also provides the physical pathway on which information flows for each service family between processes.

In Figure 8.1, completed work, represented by the folders, flows from Process A into a FIFO lane. Process B then withdraws the folders from the FIFO lane in the same order in which they entered. In other words, Process B withdraws the folders in first in, first out fashion, thus preserving the sequence of work between the processes.

Preserving the sequence of work by creating FIFO lanes is very important. It eliminates the shuffling and reprioritizing of work at each process and helps create predictability around when each job will be completed. In most offices, the constant changing of priorities means it is often very difficult to determine a date or time by which each job will be completed, and this, in turn, usually leads to additional reshuffling and reprioritization.

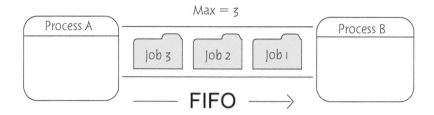

Figure 8.1 **A simple example of FIFO.**

FIFO and the Five Key Questions for Value Stream Flow in the Office

In a processing cell, it's apparent how work flows through the cell, how everyone knows what to work on next, and where to send the work once it's finished. However, when the processes are disconnected, these things are often impossible to determine without management or employees making decisions.

FIFO establishes connections between two processes or part-time processing cells. Having processes connected in FIFO enables employees to answer the five key questions for value stream flow in the office:

1. How do I know what to work on next?

2. Where do I get my work from?

3. How long should it take me to perform my work?

4. Where do I send my work?

5. When I send my work, is flow still normal?

Where FIFO exists, employees can answer all five of these questions with a simple, single answer and not with: "It depends." By fixing the sequence of work between the processes, everyone knows that its order of completion will not change, which is part of what enables employees to answer the five questions. The other part is handled via standard work, which will be covered later.

In Figure 8.2, each number shows where or how its corresponding question can be answered.

1. How do I know what to work on next? *From the FIFO lane.*

2. Where do I get my work from? *The next physical (or electronic) space in the FIFO lane.*

3. How long should it take me to perform my work? *Follow standard work.*

4. Where do I send my work? *Into the outgoing physical (or electronic) FIFO lane.*

5. When I send my work, is flow still normal? *Work would be sent to the next process once it's completed, but we will need to note whether the FIFO lane we put it in is in a normal condition or if we are placing work into an abnormal zone.*

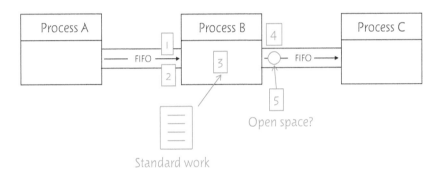

Figure 8.2 **Connecting processes with FIFO lanes enables employees to answer the five key questions for value stream flow in the office.**

What To Do When FIFO Backs Up

FIFO lanes need to have a maximum quantity of work that is designed to be in them at any point. The maximum will correspond to the takt capability under which we are operating. By establishing a maximum, we establish the threshold for designed normal flow. If we exceed the maximum, we know we have abnormal flow. If more work flows in, it does not mean we stop the flow (we wouldn't tell customers to stop requesting quotes, for example). It simply means that today something happened, normal flow has been exceeded, and we need to react.

Visual FIFO

It is important to see FIFO in the office visually, as this is a good indicator of normal versus abnormal flow. This often requires a good dose of creativity. For example, it might not be possible to physically queue files between processes because they are digital. In such cases, consider again how you can make the digital physical. Many offices create FIFO lanes that hold cards, icons, magnetic tokens, or some other representation of the work in need of completion in order to preserve its sequence. Then, as each card or icon is withdrawn, the actual work associated with the symbol is completed (Figure 8.3).

In Figure 8.3, the red zone in each individual FIFO lane indicates if abnormal flow has occurred for that service family. Note that the red zone can be different for different service families, so even though there are the same number of jobs for the *Underwriting* and *CAPEX* service families, the red zone for each is different. The flow for the *Underwriting* service family is normal, but the flow for the *CAPEX* service family is abnormal.

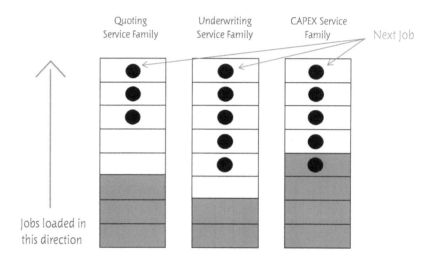

Figure 8.3 **The tokens in these FIFO lanes represent the work that needs to be completed for each service family, preserving the desired sequence through the flow. Each token may have a file name and location written on it so the person pulling the token knows where to find the related documents.**

Digital FIFO

For a variety of reasons, FIFO lanes that feed a processing cell are usually digital. These electronic FIFO lanes (e-FIFO) would operate under the same first in, first out rules as every other FIFO lane, and their purpose would also be the same.

To create e-FIFO lanes, it's often possible to use tools that are probably already part of your email operating system. It's generally possible to create "rules" around email inboxes that route information to specific inbox folders for each processing cell. The timestamp of each email in the inbox will show the order in which the work needs to be processed. For example, by putting the name of the family and name of the processing cell in the subject line, work can automatically be moved to the respective subfolder, and the inbox time will preserve the FIFO sequence (Figure 8.4).

Figure 8.4 **The tools built into an email system can be used to create electronic FIFO lanes that preserve the sequence of work per service family.**

Multiple FIFO Lanes

When a process or processing cell services multiple families, then multiple FIFO lanes are used (Figure 8.5).

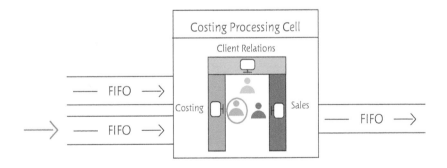

Figure 8.5 **A processing cell being fed by more than one FIFO lane. Each FIFO lane would be for a different service family.**

In Figure 8.5, the processing cell completes work for more than one service family, and each service family flows into the processing cell via a separate FIFO lane. An indicator, represented by the arrow in Figure 8.5, would be needed so the first employee in the processing cell knows which FIFO lane to take work from next without having to ask any questions or disrupt the flow.

There would need to be some established sequence in which the FIFO lanes are emptied. There are many ways of setting this sequence. It could be that one FIFO lane is emptied completely, then the other one is emptied. Or, perhaps the cell alternates between the two lanes to keep work flowing in both value streams.

Fast Track FIFO Lanes

"Fast track" FIFO lanes, or FIFO lanes created to get work through quickly and bypass existing work, can be used, but *only* if it supports our business model (e.g., if we offer an expedite service and customers pay more for it). If this is the case, then it's possible to create an expedite FIFO lane that flows into the same processes or part-time processing cells as all the other "normal" FIFO lanes.

Be careful when implementing an expedite FIFO system like this. Without firm rules around how it operates, you might quickly find everyone trying to send their work down the expedite lane. These expedite FIFO lanes would not be used to correct mistakes, enable reprioritizations, or anything else. Their existence would strictly be based on whether it's a service we offer as a competitive advantage in our business, not as a solution to other performance issues with the flow.

 Human Resources
FIFO

In our HR example with the *Technical New Hire* service family, a processing cell was created to process candidates in a process one, move one fashion from "First Interview" through "Technical Test 2." Also, a second processing cell was created for the final three processes in the flow, from "Review Final Interview Results" through "Create Offer Letter."

Helpful Hint
Keep the standard work for operating multiple FIFO lanes simple. Consider:

- *Always alternate.*
- *Would they often be full at the same time?*
- *If demand is low, would it matter much which one is chosen first?*

We will now use FIFO to connect the processing cells with the activities that supply them with work. We also will connect the individual processes together with FIFO.

Figure 8.6 shows the processes and part-time processing cells connected by FIFO lanes.

When an IT candidate passes through this flow, once the first interview has been completed, the candidate would take the first technical test, then the second technical test. If an engineering candidate is up for consideration, he or she would likewise go through the first interview and take the first technical test, but after this, the work associated with the candidate would flow directly to "Evaluate Test Results" via a FIFO lane, because engineering candidates are not required to take the second technical test.

Having more than one flow path by incorporating multiple FIFO lanes into the design ensures that the system of flow created is capable of handling both engineering and IT candidates through the same flow, even though the IT candidates take a slightly different path.

The challenging aspect of operating a multiple FIFO lane system like this comes at "Evaluate Test Results," where the two paths reconverge once again into the main flow. At this process, it has to be especially clear how people will answer the first question for flow: "How do I know what to work on next?" In this case, it would be which FIFO lane should I pull from when there is work in both? Standard work will need to be created at this process to govern how to withdraw work from which FIFO lane, in what quantity, and when. Alternating FIFO lanes is a simple approach and would work. If the company is only hiring an engineer or IT associate, but not both, only one flow path would be in use, so this would not be an issue.

The final item to be considered when connecting processes with FIFO is what to do when a FIFO lane becomes full. It's important that these lanes get "cleared" down to a minimum level to allow for erratic demand that may come in. If we leave them full, we will always be in an abnormal condition as more work arrives. To clear the FIFO lane, we may have to run the processing cell longer to get the FIFO lane back to normal conditions. We also may have to readjust the size of the FIFO lane and further investigate why the increase in demand is happening.

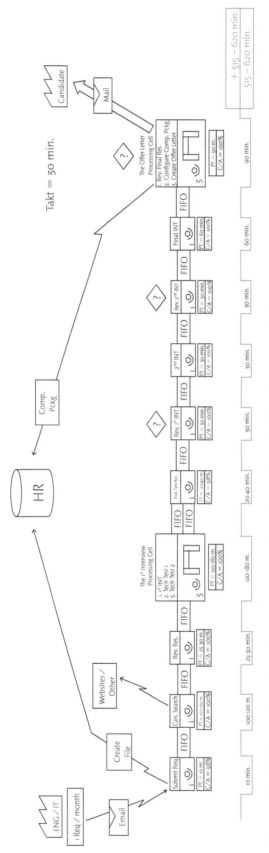

Figure 8.6 **The FIFO connections for each process or processing cell in the *Technical New Hire* service family.**

practical **Engineering**
application **FIFO**

The processing cells and activities that supply them with information in the *Moderate Customer Redesign* value stream will be connected with FIFO. We will connect the individual processes doing the work as well.

Recall the balance chart for the *Moderate Customer Redesign* service family (Figure 8.7).

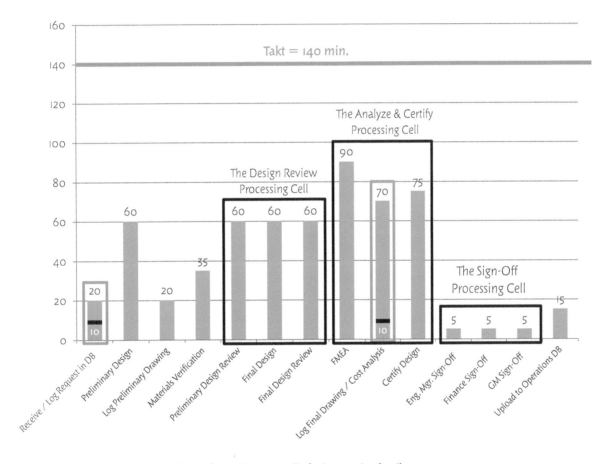

Figure 8.7 **The balance chart for the *Moderate Customer Redesign* service family.**

To begin creating FIFO connections, we need to focus initially on the first two processes, "Receive/Log Request in Database" and "Preliminary Design." Once the design work at "Preliminary Design" has been completed, the business will know whether a *Customer Redesign* falls into the *Standard, Moderate,* or *Complex* family.

From this point forward, it will be easy to distinguish the individual service families based on their total process times. Figure 8.8 shows the FIFO connections between the first two processes in the *Moderate Customer Redesign* flow.

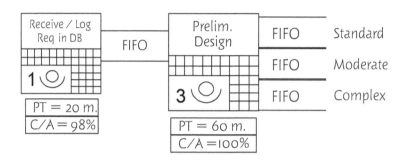

Figure 8.8 **The FIFO lanes for the first two processes in the flow.**

While work will come into "Preliminary Design" through one FIFO lane, it will leave through one of three: one FIFO lane for the *Standard* family, one FIFO lane for the *Moderate* family, and one lane for the *Complex* family.

In the full value stream map, we will only show the one FIFO lane leaving "Preliminary Design." This FIFO lane will be for the *Moderate Customer Redesign* family, because this is the only service family we are mapping. In the physical office, once the *Standard, Moderate,* and *Complex* families have *all* been implemented, there would be three physical FIFO lanes leaving "Preliminary Design."

This type of multiple FIFO lane system would need to be created if it were truly impossible to determine what type of *Customer Redesign* has been submitted before any design work had begun on it. If this knowledge could be obtained right when *Customer Redesigns* were received and logged, then each type could be loaded into its own FIFO lane *before* "Preliminary Design" and carried through on a separate FIFO track to the end of its respective flow.

Since the targeted flow is for *Moderate Customer Redesigns*, this is the FIFO track, which is shown in Figure 8.9.

The FIFO connections for all the processes and processing cells should be fairly straightforward. There are no multiple FIFO lanes. We would simply need to decide if the connections would be made physically or electronically.

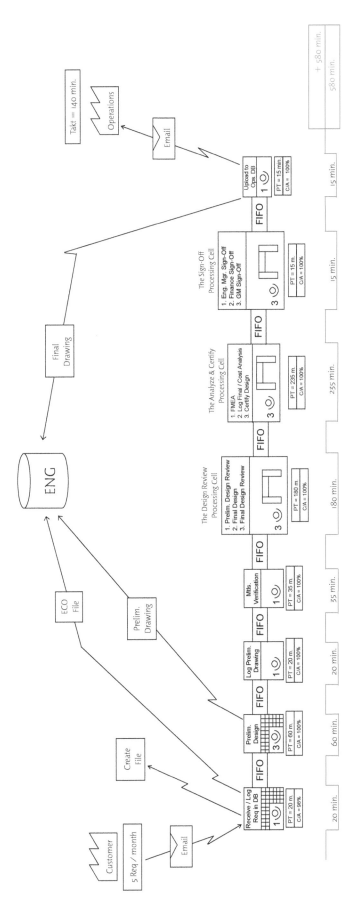

Figure 8.9 The FIFO connections for the *Moderate Customer Redesign* service family.

Action Item

Create FIFO lanes between processes and processing cells to connect them in flow.

Check off each step as it is completed.

☐ Identify how many processes and processing cells exist in the flow.

☐ Determine how to implement FIFO lanes between the processes and processing cells.

☐ If the work or files are digital in nature, determine how FIFO will regulate the sequence of work between the processes in a way that everyone will be able to see.

☐ Draw a mock-up of your FIFO lanes, complete with the maximum amount of work authorized to be in each of them.

☐ Determine if the five key questions for value stream flow in the office can be answered for each FIFO connection established.

Acid Test

The FIFO lane feeding a process should be the only way that process determines what to work on next. Ensure work in a FIFO lane cannot be rearranged or reprioritized.

Action Item
Create FIFO Lanes

1. List the processes that will be connected by FIFO.

2. For each connection, state how the FIFO lane will be presented. Physically with folders? Physically with indicators or markers? On a whiteboard with tokens? Electronically with email, digital display, or other methods?

3. If a digital display is chosen, what system will be used?

4. Explain how a visitor will be able to see if the FIFO lane is empty or full.

Note: If needed, copy this page for the remaining FIFO connections in the value stream.

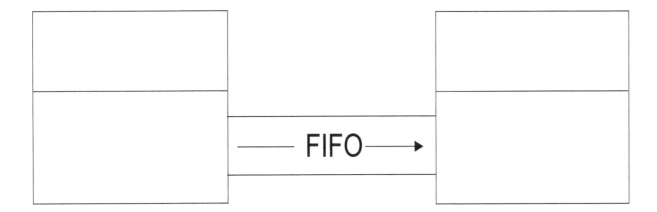

Describe the FIFO Lanes Created

Processes or cells connected

_____

_____

_____

Digital or physical FIFO

_____

_____

_____

How the FIFO lane and the work it holds will be made visual

_____

_____

_____

FIFO maximum

_____

_____

_____

Visual indicator for when abnormal flow occurs

_____

_____

_____

How do I know what to work on next?

_____

_____

_____

Where do I get my work from?

_____

_____

_____

Describe the FIFO Lanes Created (Continued)

How long should it take me to perform my work?

_____

_____

_____

Where do I send my work?

_____

_____

_____

When I send my work, is flow still normal?

_____

_____

_____

Notes

_____

_____

_____

chapter nine

Guideline #4: Workflow Cycles

Workflow cycles refer to the rate at which work moves or flows within or between different work areas or departments along a fixed pathway. They dictate the time by which work should be completed and help stabilize the flow of information in the office. Workflow cycles are one of the most powerful concepts in the office, because when they are set up correctly, they yield a *guaranteed turnaround time* (GTT) for the flow of the service family.

Having a GTT means we can turn around or provide the requested information within a set amount of time, e.g., in by Monday at noon, out by Tuesday at 10 a.m.—guaranteed. Guaranteed turnaround times are a crucial element to creating flow in the office. They eliminate chasing information, status meetings,

reprioritizations, phone calls, emails, and many more activities that disrupt information flow.

Workflow cycles play a major role in successfully creating guaranteed turnaround times in the office. They ensure that information flows at predetermined intervals and they also denote a key point for capturing useful knowledge, which are the two key functions of an office.

Workflow cycles do more than create flow between processes. They dictate when processing cells will meet, when FIFO lanes will be emptied, when workers will perform work at their processes, when information will be provided to the next process, and when information will be delivered

Definition

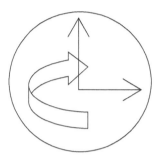

Guaranteed turnaround time means that the time it takes to flow work through an area of the value stream, or perhaps the complete value stream, is predictable, repeatable, dependable, and reliable.

to the customer in a predictable, reliable manner. This builds credibility and dependability with the customer, which is good for business growth.

Figure 9.1 shows the symbol used to identify where and when workflow cycles will occur.

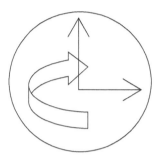

Figure 9.1 **The symbol used for a workflow cycle.**

Levels of Workflow Cycles

Not only do workflow cycles create guaranteed turnaround times for the flow of information, they also happen at many levels. A workflow cycle might happen at an individual process through the use of an individual calendar (Figure 9.2).

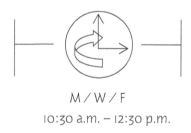

M / W / F
10:30 a.m. – 12:30 p.m.

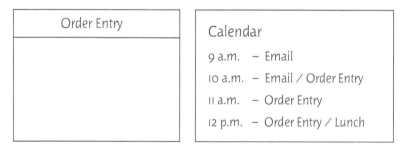

Figure 9.2 **A workflow cycle created for "Order Entry" using an individual calendar.**

Workflow cycles might happen as well at processing cells, where multiple individual processes complete work in process one, move one fashion. The example seen in Figure 9.3 indicates that work will flow in this processing cell from 1 p.m. to 4 p.m. every Monday, Wednesday, and Friday.

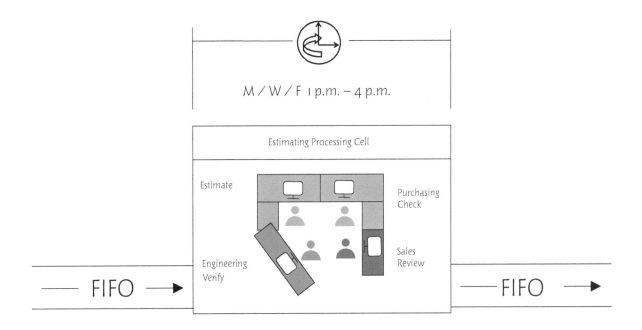

M / W / F 1 p.m. – 4 p.m.

Figure 9.3 **A workflow cycle governing when and for how long the part-time processing cell meets.**

Workflow cycles also can establish a guaranteed turnaround time for more than one process or processing cell. Figure 9.4 shows workflow cycles governing when work will flow from "Order Entry" to the FIFO (first in, first out) lane feeding the processing cell. In this case, that would happen every Monday, Wednesday, and Friday by 12:30 p.m., then the processing cell would begin its work at 1 p.m. on the same days. This means that any order entry work that commences at 10:30 a.m. on Monday, Wednesday, and Friday would be processed by the processing cell by 4 p.m. on Monday, Wednesday, and Friday.

Helpful Hint

The importance of workflow cycles is that they create a GTT. Use these GTTs when interfacing with other areas of the company. Once established and reliable, use them with customers, too.

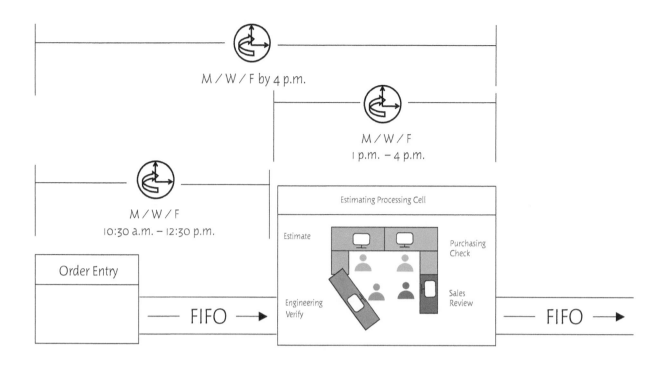

M / W / F by 4 p.m.

M / W / F
1 p.m. – 4 p.m.

M / W / F
10:30 a.m. – 12:30 p.m.

Order Entry

—— FIFO ——→

Estimating Processing Cell

Estimate

Purchasing Check

Engineering Verify

Sales Review

—— FIFO ——→

Figure 9.4 **The top workflow cycle and guaranteed turnaround time govern the timing for the flow that starts at the beginning of "Order Entry" and ends with the conclusion of the part-time processing cell for estimating.**

Figure 9.5 shows what a workflow cycle and guaranteed turnaround time would look like for an entire end-to-end flow, from initialization to delivery of the service to the customer.

Workflow Cycles and Multiple FIFO Lanes

Workflow cycles also can be used to govern when to withdraw and process work from a multiple FIFO lane system (Figure 9.6).

Each Monday, Wednesday, and Friday, work would be withdrawn and processed from the purple FIFO lane at 1 p.m. On Tuesdays and Thursdays, work would be withdrawn and processed from the blue FIFO lane at 9 a.m. All completed work would be put into the black outgoing FIFO lane, regardless of where it originated.

Using workflow cycles in this way can help avoid decision making when a process or processing cell is being fed by more than one FIFO lane.

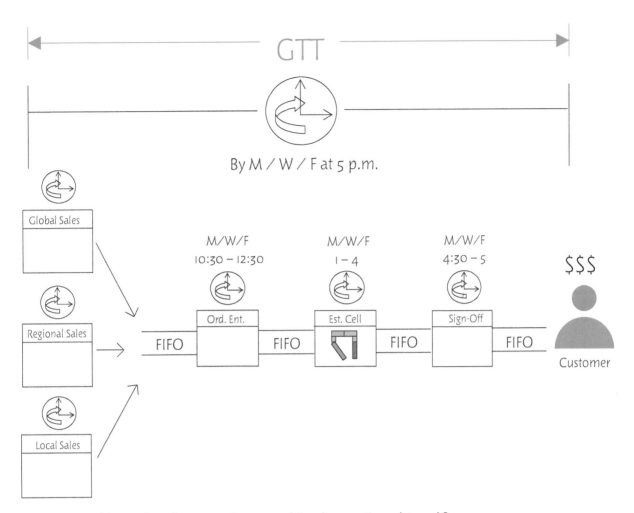

Figure 9.5 **A workflow cycle and guaranteed turnaround time for an entire end-to-end flow.**

Workflow Cycles and Calendars

Workflow cycles should be marked on the calendar of each employee involved with the service. With blocks of time marked off for the workflow cycle and other blocks open or free for the completion of other work or responsibilities, it will be clear when the flow is supposed to happen and when other work is supposed to be completed. An example of an employee calendar can be seen in Figure 9.7.

In terms of staffing processing cells, it's a good idea to have everyone present during the entire time the processing cell is in session. Participants can bring other work to complete until they need to work in flow. This will ensure that if any questions arise during the workflow cycle, these employees will be present to answer them, which will reduce handoffs and waiting.

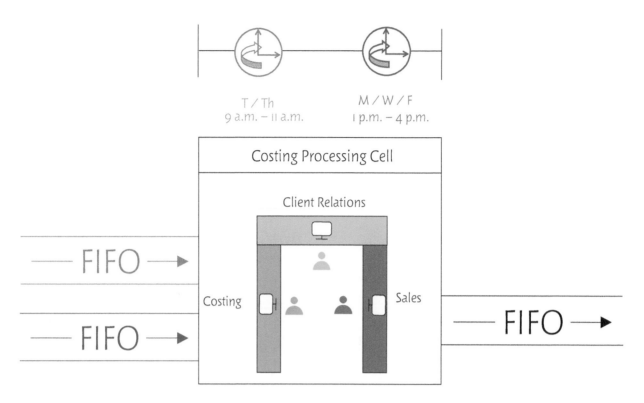

Figure 9.6 **Different workflow cycles can be used to govern when work is taken and processed from multiple FIFO lanes.**

Scheduling Workflow Cycles: Two Options

There are two primary ways to schedule or set up workflow cycles: either *fixed* or *triggered*.

Fixed workflow cycles occur with regular frequency, i.e., at the same time and on the same day of the week, every week. Triggered workflow cycles do not become activated until a specific triggering event in the value stream takes place.

Helpful Hint

Wherever possible, use a visible signal to indicate that a workflow cycle is in progress. This could be a sign on the meeting room door where a part-time dedicated processing cell is in action, or it could be a person putting up a sign on her computer saying something along the lines of: "Please do not disturb. I am participating in a workflow cycle." Visual signals such as these protect the flow, spread the message, and build cultural buy-in to the new way of operating (Figure 9.8).

	Monday	Tuesday	Wednesday	Thursday	Friday
8 am					
9 am		Quick Quote Cell		Quick Quote Cell	
10 am	Med. Quote Cell	Med. Quote Cell	Med. Quote Cell	Med. Quote Cell	Med. Quote Cell
11 am					
12 pm	Lunch	Lunch	Lunch	Lunch	Lunch
1 pm					
2 pm					
3 pm		Complex Quote Cell	Complex Quote Cell		Complex Quote Cell
4 pm					
5 pm					

Figure 9.7 **An example employee calendar showing open time and times marked off for working in the different quote processing cells.**

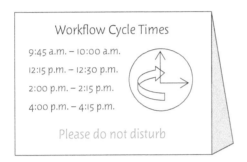

Figure 9.8 **This sign indicates that an employee is working within a workflow cycle and would be hung on the employee's office door.**

A triggered workflow cycle is used in the following instances:

1. The demand for the value stream is infrequent, meaning it is not always "running" and providing its service.

2. There is unavoidable uncertainty surrounding when a process or processing cell will be able to process its work, due to either internal or external factors.

Figure 9.9 shows a fixed workflow cycle that happens with the same timing and frequency all the time.

Figure 9.10 shows a triggered workflow cycle that will only happen once the value stream has been operating for five days. On days one to four, other office processes are completing the work required for this process to flow its work on the fifth day.

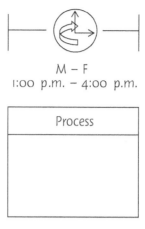

M – F
1:00 p.m. – 4:00 p.m.

Process

Figure 9.9 **This fixed workflow cycle happens every day from 1 p.m. to 4 p.m.**

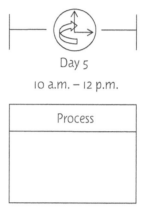

Day 5

10 a.m. – 12 p.m.

Process

Figure 9.10 **A triggered workflow cycle that does not happen regularly but occurs five days after the value stream has been initialized.**

Sizing FIFO Lanes

Once the timing of each workflow cycle has been determined for each process and processing cell in the value stream, we can size the FIFO connections between them. The size of each FIFO lane will depend on the frequency with which the workflow cycles occur at the processes or processing cells on either side of it.

A FIFO lane connecting two processes that have workflow cycles occurring every day would need to hold *at least* one day worth of work. There will be times when variation will be present in the value stream, but the process supplying the FIFO lane with work will not stop feeding it. Therefore, sizing the FIFO lane at one day is a *minimum* and we would target one and a half days to allow flexibility in the flow and the capability to handle variation when it occurs (Figure 9.11).

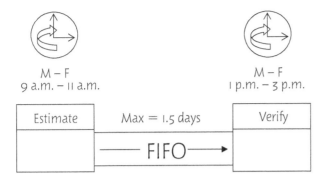

Figure 9.11 The FIFO lane would be sized to hold one and a half days worth of work, even though the workflow cycles occur every day.

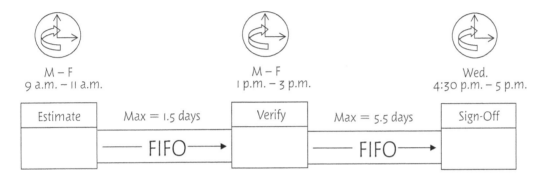

Figure 9.12 The FIFO lane connecting "Verify" and "Sign-Off" will hold five and a half days worth of work because the workflow cycle for the "Sign-Off" process only happens once a week.

If workflow cycles do not occur every day, then we need to increase the size of the FIFO lane to accommodate the reduced frequency. In Figure 9.12, the "Sign-Off" process only occurs once per week. Even though the "Verify" process meets every day, the FIFO lane connecting them would need to be sized to hold a minimum of five days worth of work, as the "Sign-Off" process will only empty the FIFO lane once every five days. We would size this FIFO lane at five and a half days to account for when variation occurs in the value stream.

practical application Human Resources Workflow Cycles

After we have determined where the processing cells will occur in the *Technical New Hire* value stream, the next step is to create workflow cycles and connect them to the processing cells through FIFO lanes. In the *Technical New Hire* value stream, workflow cycles will set the timing for when the work will flow as well as the physical pathway the work will follow.

The overall flow for the *Technical New Hire* service family is depicted in Figure 9.13.

Each process here is connected to the other via FIFO, and there is a part-time processing cell near the middle of the flow as well as at the very end. The engineering and IT flow paths diverge after the first technical test and converge at "Evaluate Test Results" once the IT candidates have taken the second technical test.

When creating workflow cycles, we need to structure them chronologically in the order of value stream flow to ensure a downstream process is not set up to take care of work that hasn't yet been processed upstream. Therefore, we will start where the service is initialized and work our way downstream to create the workflow cycles. We also will design the workflow cycles to happen often enough to meet the first takt capability that satisfies 80 percent of normal conditions, or one engineering or IT new hire per month.

For the *Technical New Hire* service family, there are two options to consider for creating workflow cycles. The first option involves setting up workflow cycles that occur on specific days of the week in a repeatable, predictable way. These would be *fixed* workflow cycles and could occur on the same day every week at a certain time. The next process in the flow also would have a corresponding workflow cycle that would happen perhaps every Thursday at a certain time. Fixed workflow cycles are a good option when the flow is repeatable and predictable.

The second option involves creating workflow cycles that happen after a specific triggering event. For example, once work reaches a certain portion of the flow, a "Day 1" workflow cycle would be triggered at that process. Then, perhaps three days after this "Day 1" workflow cycle has been completed, the next process or part-time processing cell would convene with a "Day 4" workflow cycle. For these processes, which do not always have a fixed and repeatable day on which they happen, we will use *triggered* workflow cycles.

Both options can be used in the same flow, because they are able to handle differences in the frequency with which various processes will need to occur. For example, the "Candidate Search" and "Review Resume" processes might need to happen multiple times before enough qualified candidates have been found to warrant conducting the first round of interviews.

Therefore, a workflow cycle will be created that happens at preset, predictable times each week until a sufficient number of qualified candidates has been

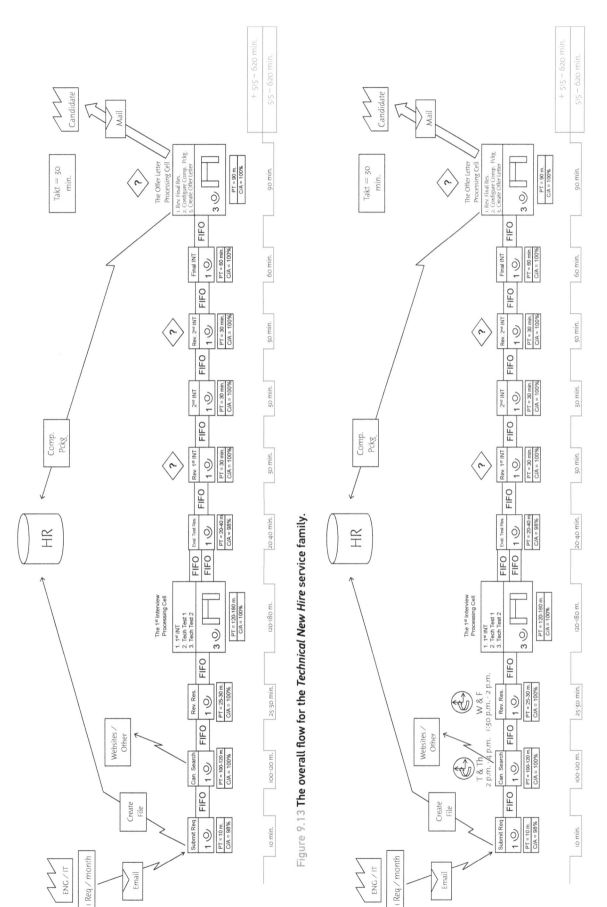

Figure 9.13 **The overall flow for the *Technical New Hire* service family.**

Figure 9.14 **The fixed workflow cycles for "Candidate Search" and "Review Resume."**

found. Once this happens, we can use triggered workflow cycles from the first interview onward (Figure 9.14).

The workflow cycles created are sufficient to cover both candidate types. When dealing with the shorter process time of the IT candidates, the workflow cycle can simply be ended earlier than it would be for the engineering candidates.

Working downstream, we will next consider the First Interview Processing Cell and the "Evaluate Test Results" process (Figure 9.15).

Knowing that we are planning for one new hire per month, it's important to understand how many *applicants* will be considered in order to hire one candidate. The business always likes to interview at least five candidates for a position. Because the process time for "First Interview" is 60 minutes and there will be five candidates (which are "the work" in this case), the total process time will be 300 minutes, meaning the workflow cycle will need to be at least 5 hours long. After the first interview, candidates proceed directly to the technical tests. The workflow cycle created for the First Interview Processing Cell needs to be long enough to cover the time needed for the tests, too. Therefore, the workflow cycle will need to be 7 hours total in length, as each technical test takes one hour to complete and IT candidates need to take both (Figure 9.16).

If there are more than five candidates for this process, perhaps if the field of applicants is particularly well qualified, the workflow cycle for the processing cell could start earlier or be extended as needed.

Once the First Interview Processing Cell has completed its work, the test results are evaluated. At "Evaluate Test Results," there are now two FIFO lanes that potentially need to be taken care of if both engineering and IT candidates are being considered at the same time. If this were the case, we would need two separate workflow cycles with different timing. However, right now, we are only creating workflow cycles for the first takt capability, in which either an engineering or IT candidate is hired (but not both). Therefore, we can create one workflow cycle that covers the timing for the longer of the two candidate types and simply not run the workflow cycle for as long when the other candidate type is up for consideration. To allow time for the workflow cycle to run longer when there are more candidates, the workflow cycle for "Evaluate Test Results" would need to take place on the next day (Figure 9.17). If engineering candidates are processed, then the appropriate engineering manager would need to be

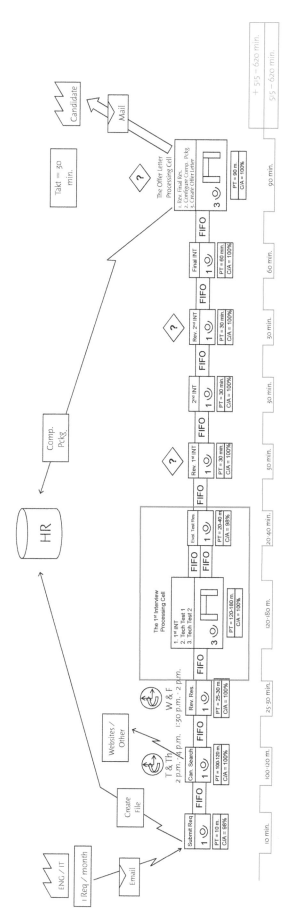

Figure 9.15 The next section of the flow for which workflow cycles need to be created.

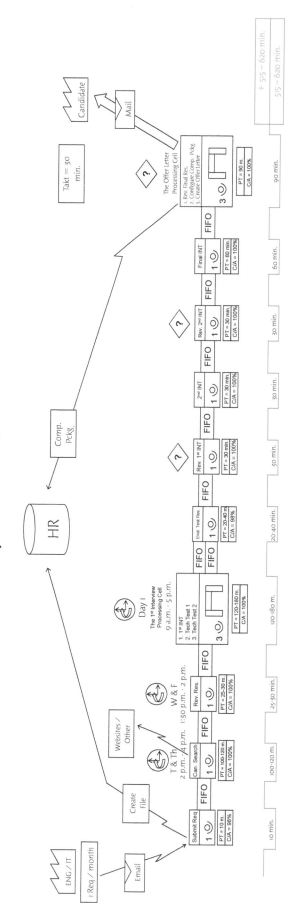

Figure 9.16 The workflow cycle at the First Interview Processing Cell is the first triggered workflow cycle and happens at the first interview process. Note that the seven-hour workflow cycle actually takes eight hours to complete, as it runs over an hour-long lunch break.

present to review the engineering test results, while someone from IT would need to be present to review the IT test results.

Continuing downstream, the next workflow cycle would take place at "Review First Interview Results." All candidates' information will proceed through this process, regardless of their test results (Figure 9.18).

Once the first interview results have been reviewed and a decision made as to who qualifies for the second round of interviews, a workflow cycle would be needed to dictate when these second interviews would take place. We will allow five days for the second interviews to be scheduled (Figure 9.19).

At "Review Second Interview Results," a decision would need to be made as to how many candidates continue on in the flow. We want to review the interview results while the information is still fresh, so we will run this work-flow cycle on the same day the second interviews are conducted (Figure 9.20).

Moving downstream, we will next create a workflow cycle for "Final Inter-view." In terms of scheduling candidates for their final interviews, we will again plan for five days to align the schedules of all the candidates and match their availability on the same day (Figure 9.21).

Once the final interview is completed, the next step is to review the results, configure a compensation package, and create and mail the offer letter in the Offer Letter Processing Cell. We can connect this processing cell to the final interview process with a workflow cycle, but should allow for extra interview time if needed. Therefore, we will run the workflow cycle for the Offer Letter Processing Cell on the following day (Figure 9.22).

Sizing FIFO Lanes

With the timing of the workflow cycles set, it's now possible to size the FIFO lanes connecting each process (Figure 9.23). Each FIFO lane has been sized slightly higher than its bare minimum to allow for variation to be absorbed by the value stream when it occurs. When workflow cycles happen close together in time, e.g., "Second Interview" and "Review Second Interview Results" on day eight, then the FIFO lane will be smaller.

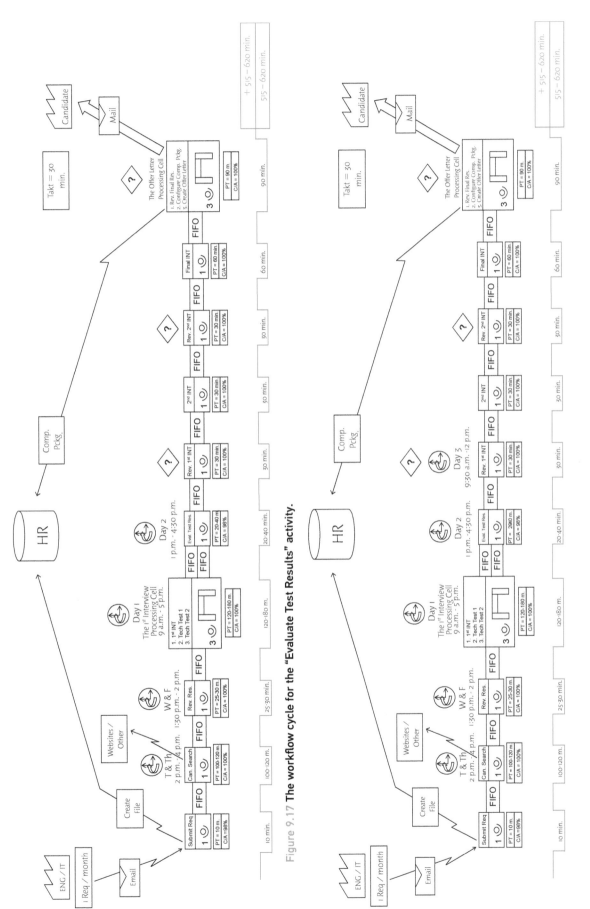

Figure 9.17 The workflow cycle for the "Evaluate Test Results" activity.

Figure 9.18 The triggered workflow cycle for the "Review First Interview Results" process.

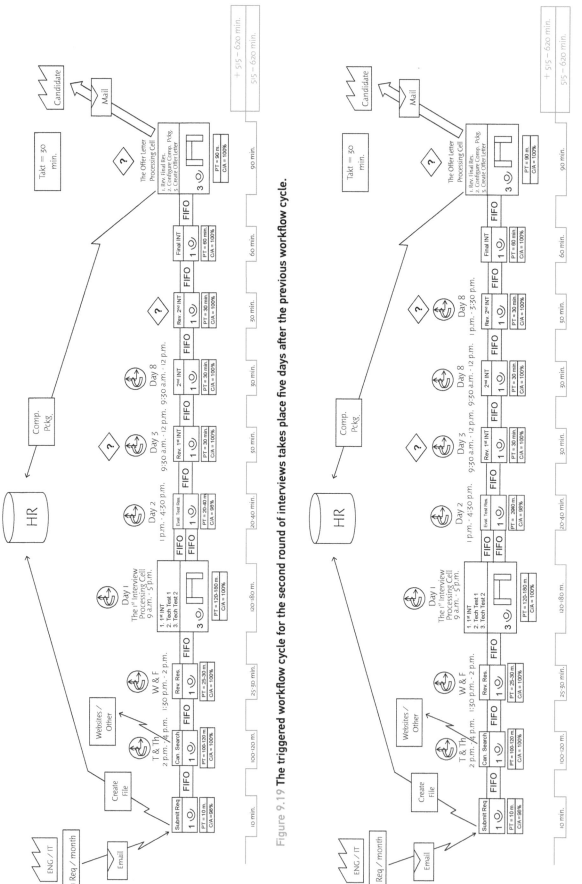

Figure 9.19 **The triggered workflow cycle for the second round of interviews takes place five days after the previous workflow cycle.**

Figure 9.20 **The triggered workflow cycle for "Review Second Interview Results," which takes place on the same day that the second interviews are conducted.**

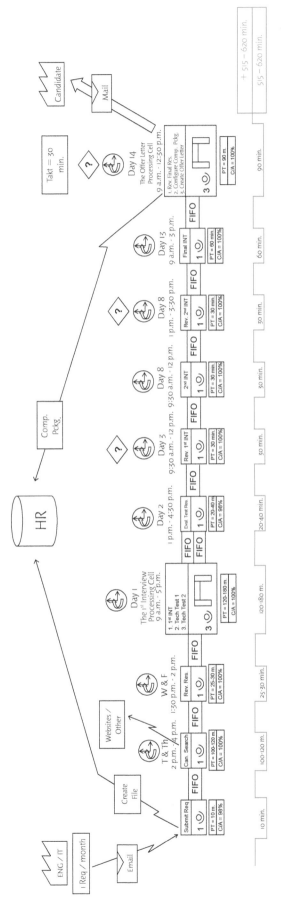

Figure 9.21 The triggered workflow cycle for the "Final Interview" process. Note that the time allotted for this workflow cycle represents the maximum amount of time possible and would only be the case if all five candidates made it this far.

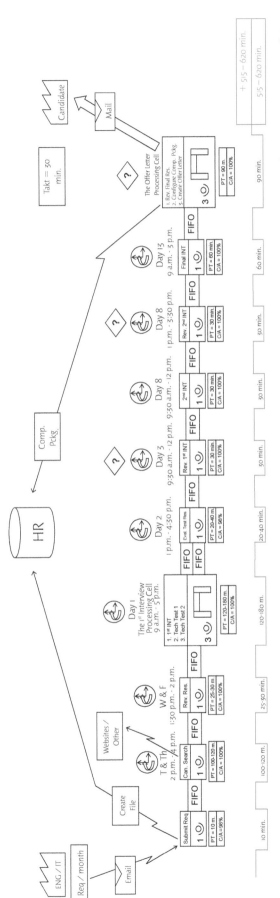

Figure 9.22 The final triggered workflow cycle in the value stream for the Offer Letter Processing Cell.

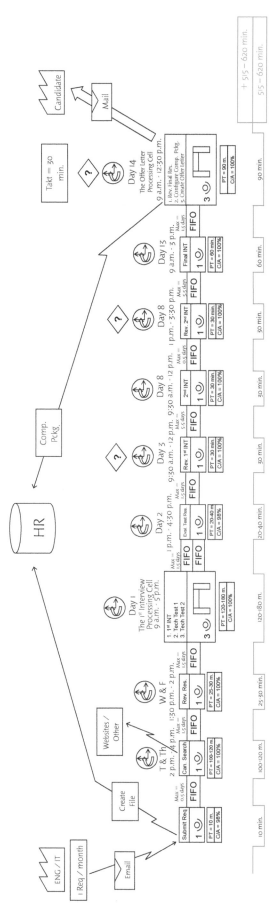

Figure 9.23 **The FIFO connections sized slightly higher than the bare minimum required.**

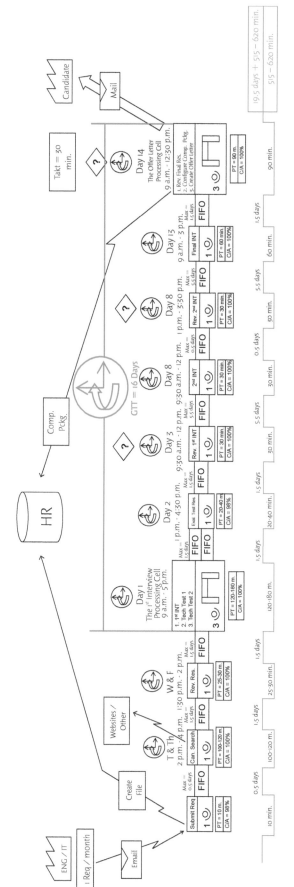

Figure 9.24 **From the first interview to mailing the offer letter, the guaranteed turnaround time is 16 days for the** *Technical New Hire* **value stream.**

The *Technical New Hire* GTT

With a workflow cycle set up for every process in the flow, it's now possible to determine a guaranteed turnaround time for the entire flow. This GTT extends from the start of the workflow cycle for the First Interview Processing Cell through the completion of the workflow cycle for the Offer Letter Processing Cell at the very end of the flow and is 16 days long (Figure 9.24). Even though the workflow cycles will be completed in only 14 days, the FIFO lanes have been sized a bit larger than the bare minimum required, which is why the GTT is 16 days.

Even though we have a GTT, we need to track the progress of the flow, and there are many ways to do this. We could create a drawing of the flow similar to Figure 9.24 and use a magnetic arrow or some other movable token to indicate where the work currently is in the flow. When hiring for multiple positions at the same time, color-coding the different tokens can differentiate each candidate as they proceed through the flow.

Sequencing the candidates in the flow can be important as well when both types are being hired. It may be best to process all the engineering candidates through a process at the same time, then all the IT candidates, or vice versa, so the employees doing the reviews are not constantly swapping in and out of the same process.

practical application Engineering **Workflow Cycles**

In Engineering, we will use the same approach as Human Resources, working in chronological order starting at the beginning and moving downstream.

The first process at which a workflow cycle will occur is "Preliminary Design." Before this, *Customer Redesigns* of all types are received by the business and logged into the company's system, and this will happen randomly whenever customers decide to send them.

Helpful Hint

For employee engagement, having the people who do the work move the magnets or physically track the work can help build ownership.

At "Preliminary Design," daily triage will happen with a fixed workflow cycle starting at 8:30 a.m. to decide which value stream will flow work (Figure 9.25).

At "Preliminary Design," employees will begin their designs and evaluate which requests fall into which *Customer Redesign* category: *Standard, Moderate,* or *Complex.* Requests determined to be *Moderate Customer Redesigns* will be placed into the corresponding FIFO lane for this family. From there, they will be processed according to the triggered workflow cycle for "Log Preliminary Drawing," as seen in Figure 9.26

Because the process time of the first workflow cycle is low, the next workflow cycle for "Materials Verification" can run later on the same day (Figure 9.27).

The next triggered workflow cycle for the Design Review Processing Cell will take place on the next day, because the process time for the processing cell is too long to fit in on the first day (Figure 9.28).

To account for the range of time needed in the design process, an extra day has been allowed in the flow by placing the next triggered workflow cycle for the Analyze & Certify Processing Cell on the fourth day (Figure 9.29). This will allow for the completion of any designs that required a little more time without disrupting the GTT of the overall flow.

The triggered workflow cycle for the Sign-Off Processing Cell could take place on day four as well, but again, it's important to allow for the range of designs that are needed by placing this workflow cycle on day five. Over time, we could observe the FIFO lane and note how work is flowing, and this extra day could be removed if not needed (Figure 9.30).

It's important that there is as little time as possible between the workflow cycle for the Sign-Off Processing Cell and uploading the information to the Operations database. Therefore, the timing of the "Upload to Operations DB" workflow cycle has been structured to occur two hours after the previous workflow cycle concludes (Figure 9.31).

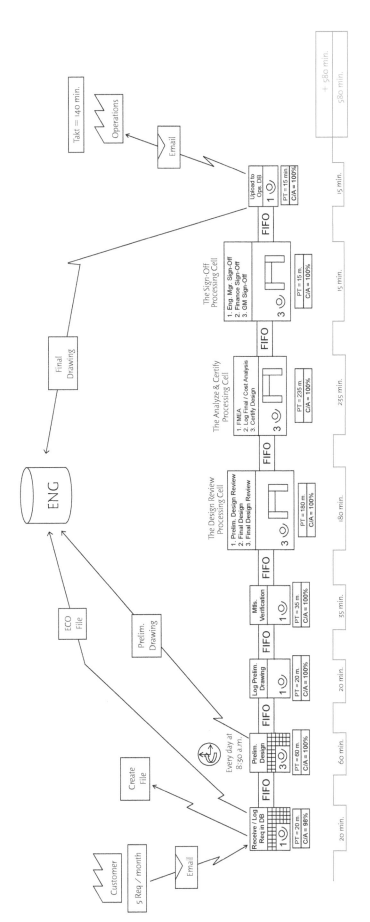

Figure 9.25 Triage will happen via a fixed workflow cycle first thing every day at "Preliminary Design."

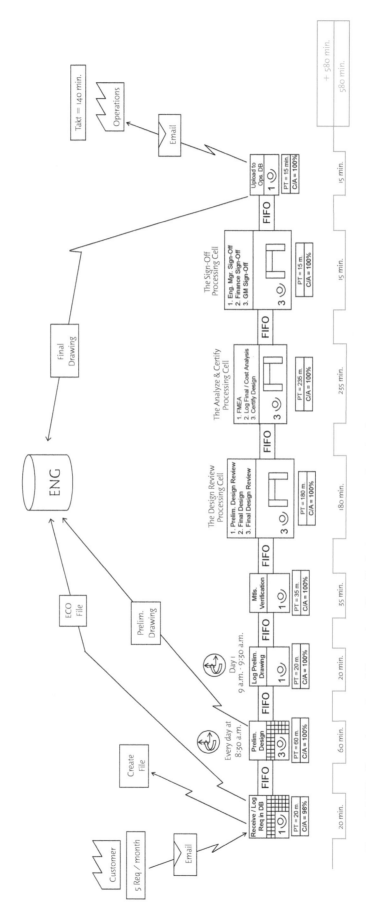

Figure 9.26 The first triggered workflow cycle at "Log Preliminary Drawing" marks the starting point for the GTT for *Moderate Customer Redesigns*.

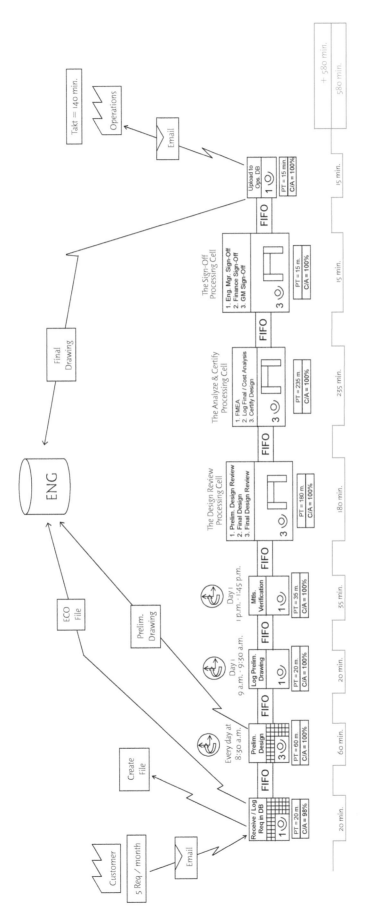

Figure 9.27 The triggered workflow cycle for "Materials Verification."

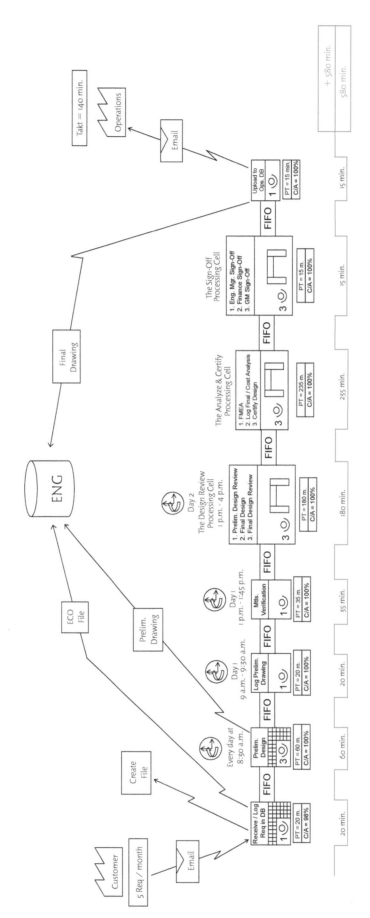

Figure 9.28 **The triggered workflow cycle for the Design Review Processing Cell.**

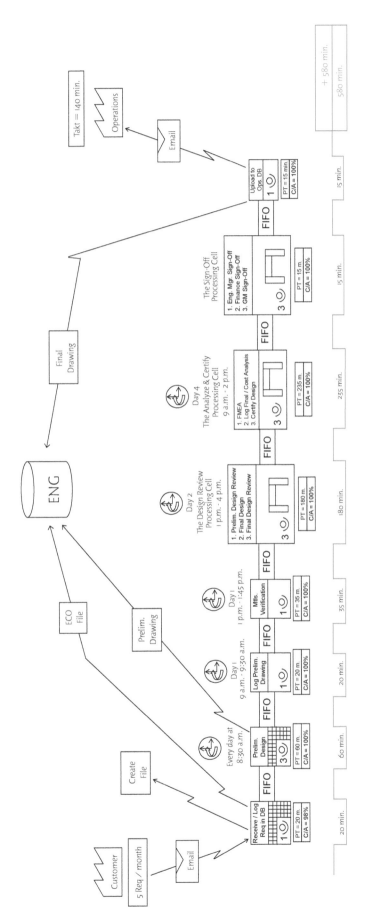

Figure 9.29 The triggered workflow cycle for the Analyze & Certify Processing Cell.

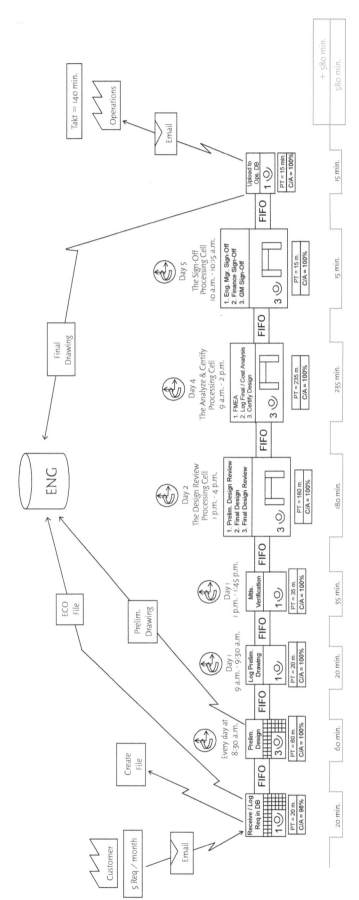

Figure 9.30 The triggered workflow cycle for the Sign-Off Processing Cell takes place on day five.

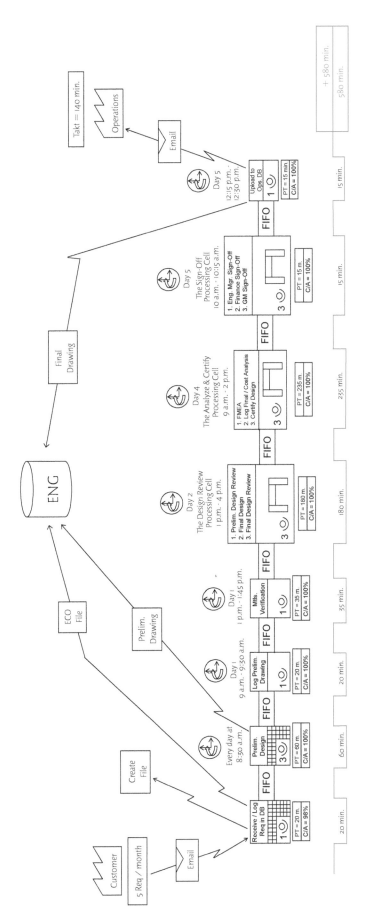

Figure 9.31 **The workflow cycles for the *Moderate Customer Redesign* service family.**

Sizing FIFO Lanes

With the timing of the workflow cycles set, the FIFO lanes connecting each process and processing cell can be sized. While some FIFO lanes are designed to allow work to accumulate, when the workflow cycles are close together in time, the FIFO lane will be smaller, as is the case for the FIFO lane connecting the Sign-Off Processing Cell with "Upload to Operations DB" (Figure 9.32).

The *Moderate Customer Redesign* GTT

As a result of the processing cells, workflow cycles, and FIFO lanes, the GTT for the flow is eight and a half days from the FIFO lane before the "Log Preliminary Drawing" workflow cycle to the "Upload to Operations DB" workflow cycle (Figure 9.33). We factor in the FIFO lane to the GTT because this is the first point in the value stream where we will know we are dealing with *Moderate Customer Redesigns*.

Although the workflow cycles will effectively run five days, the GTT is eight and a half days because the FIFO lanes have been sized to hold more than the minimum amount of work required to allow for variation in the types of designs requested.

The GTT also will provide predictability and stability to the Moderate Customer Redesign service family and eliminate chasing information, phone calls, emails, and meetings.

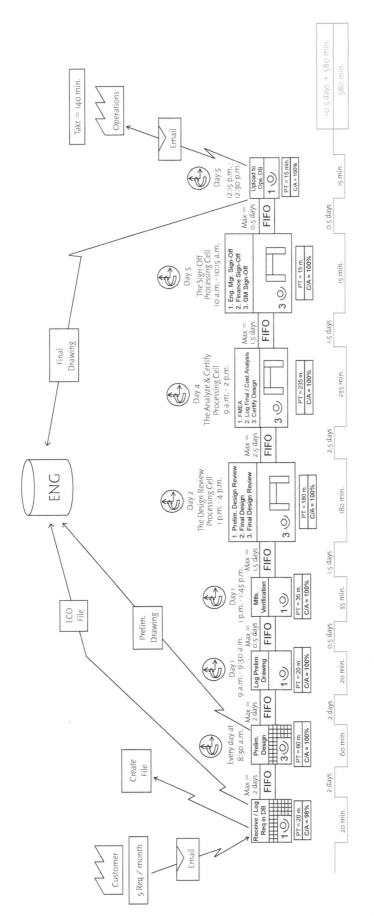

Figure 9.32 The FIFO connections sized between each process and processing cell.

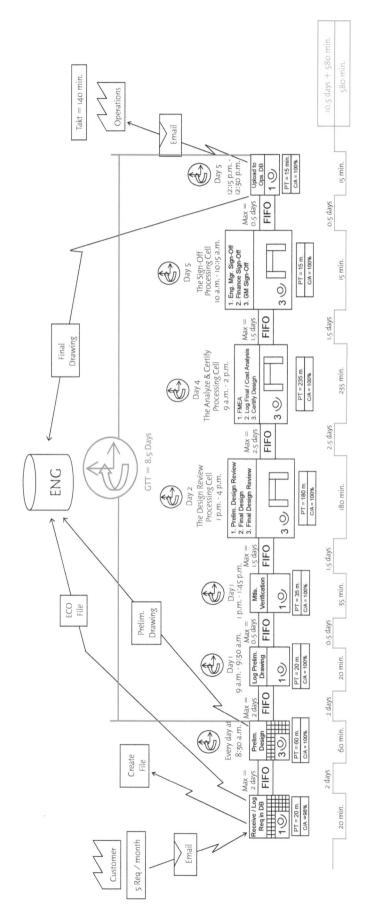

Figure 9.33 The guaranteed turnaround time for the *Moderate Customer Redesign* value stream.

Action Item

· ·

Create workflow cycles for each processing cell and process in the flow, and create employee calendars that show time blocked off for workflow cycles and time blocked off as open for the completion of other work and responsibilities.

Check off each step as it is completed.

☐ Create a workflow cycle for each processing cell and process in the flow.

☐ Determine the timing of each workflow cycle based on the established takt or takt capability.

☐ Size each FIFO lane based on the frequency with which the workflow cycles of the processes or processing cells before and after it will process the work.

☐ From the workflow cycles created, determine a guaranteed turnaround time (GTT) for the overall, end-to-end flow that is fixed and predictable.

☐ Create employee calendars showing certain blocks of time dedicated to completing workflow cycles and other blocks of time open for the completion of other work and responsibilities.

Acid Test

· ·

The timing of when work will move through each process or processing cell is clear. Each process or processing cell knows when to expect information from the preceding process or processing cell.

Action Item
Create Workflow Cycles

1.　Name the processes or cells.

2.　Determine if the workflow cycles will be fixed or triggered.

3.　Name the workflow cycles.

4.　Size the FIFO lane based on the frequency with which the workflow cycles will meet.

5.　Determine a guaranteed turnaround time for the overall, end-to-end flow.

Note: If needed, copy this page for the remaining workflow cycles determined.

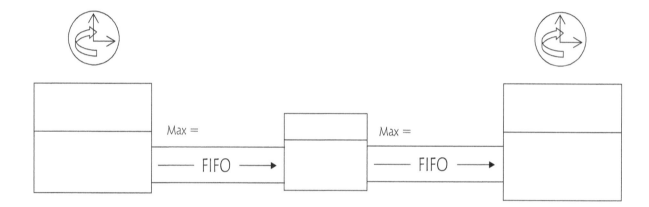

Action Item
Create Employee Calendars

Employee Name: _____

	Monday	Tuesday	Wednesday	Thursday	Friday
8 am					
9 am					
10 am					
11 am					
12 pm					
1 pm					
2 pm					
3 pm					
4 pm					
5 pm					

Employee Name: _____

	Monday	Tuesday	Wednesday	Thursday	Friday
8 am					
9 am					
10 am					
11 am					
12 pm					
1 pm					
2 pm					
3 pm					
4 pm					
5 pm					

Describe the Workflow Cycles Created

Name of processes or cells

_____

_____

_____

Workflow cycle name

_____

_____

_____

Starting process and ending process

_____

_____

_____

Day of the week the workflow cycle meets

_____

_____

_____

Time the workflow cycle meets

_____

_____

_____

Guaranteed turnaround time for the end-to-end flow

_____

_____

_____

Notes

_____

_____

_____

chapter
ten

Guideline #5: Integration Events

Workflow cycles are used to flow work on a consistent or regular basis. However, work may not *need* to flow on a regular basis. It may only need to flow every quarter, when a new product launches, or when we need to send information to an outside service.

In these situations, a large amount of information is typically "handed off." When handing off a large amount of work from one area of the company to another area or to an outside service on an irregular or "as needed" basis, we would use an *integration event.**

Integration events usually require information from several different areas of the company prior to handing off the information to the next phase of flow. To address this, one of the key elements in an integration event is matching outputs to inputs, which means that the receiving parties would receive the information in the exact format they need. For example, if a spreadsheet was provided, the receiving party would not have to manipulate the data any further by creating a pivot table or a graph from the data that was handed over.

To match outputs with inputs, the sending and receiving parties would meet and review in detail how the receiving party will use the information, what format they would need it in, and then create a "checklist" to ensure that when they send the information it is all there and in the format required.

*Integration events were first used in product development. Kennedy, M. N. 2003. *Product Development for the Lean Enterprise.* Richmond, VA: The Oaklea Press.

Integration events are also the formal place designated to capture knowledge. This knowledge could be captured in the form of binders, databases, spreadsheets, or many other forms, as long as it is accessible going forward to assist in the processing of future customer requests. Capturing knowledge also means including research and data that were developed even if they were not used in the final development of the product or service. For example, a cost analysis may determine the best choice for selecting a material, but with that knowledge should be the research on other choices as well. Presenting knowledge in the form of tradeoff curves, showing different attributes on a curve and where the curve of each intersects, is a good method for presenting a large amount of knowledge in a concise manner.

In a small, one-site office, you could use physical binders to formally capture knowledge. However, in today's digital age, it's more likely you will need to enter the knowledge into a global database. At the integration event, information would be presented in the manner that fits the data entry exactly. All information would be presented in the format needed in order for the knowledge to be captured for future use. No calculations would be needed or interpretation of data, and all information needed would be available to the person entering the data without any assistance needed.

While integration events are sometimes similar to milestone events that are set up to drive projects to dates, they, in fact, are different. When driving to meet milestones, managers set priorities, negotiate with other departments and services, adjust resources, reprioritize, and, most of all, optimize their respective areas, including how they will deliver the best information.

With integration events, work is performed in workflow cycles, which means it is done in flow to achieve the date needed, or work on a project is being done between the workflow cycles. In either case, there is time and resources allotted for the work needed before the integration event takes place, and, by putting that work in the format the receiving party needs, we save a lot of time and rework after the event happens.

Integration events require that the format of the information has been
determined and a checklist developed. Therefore, each sending party
knows the format of the information required and no further negotiation
by management is needed.

As seen in Table 10.1, we can summarize the differences between milestone
events and integration events.

Table 10.1 **Summarizing the differences between milestone events and integration events**

Milestone Events	Integration Events
Management drives individuals to make dates.	Workflow cycles move information to dates.
Individuals provide work in the format that was easiest for them.	Outputs match inputs in a preestablished format.
Information provided can be negotiated.	No negotiation.
Information is reworked.	There is a checklist of information needed.
Clarification is needed on the information.	No clarification is needed.
Milestone meetings turn into discussions where decisions are made and direction is set.	No decisions are made, no direction is set.
There is no format used to capture knowledge.	Formal place to capture knowledge.
Often there is a follow-up event needed to check all the rework and reformatting.	No follow-up meetings are needed.

Helpful Hint

*To help match outputs with inputs, it may help to review what has happened in the past when information was
handed over. How many phone calls were placed looking for clarification? How many follow-up emails were sent
and what information were they seeking? Why were meetings held to review information after it was handed over?
All of these will lead to developing a more robust integration event.*

Figure 10.1 shows the symbol used for an integration event.

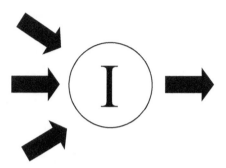

Figure 10.1 **The symbol used for an integration event.**

A true integration event could be as simple as the receiving party waiting in a room at the time of the event. They would have with them a binder that contains a prelabeled section for each input they need to receive from the other areas of the company. The sending parties would all come in at the time of the event, and, after a greeting and a brief introduction on the purpose of the event, the receiving person would hold out his/her hand to take a package from the first sending party. They discuss a few things about the information inside, but it would be a light discussion and the package would not have to be opened or reviewed. The receiving party would simply drop it into his/her binder under the appropriate tab and then continue to do this for the remaining sending parties in the room until the binder is complete.

Figure 10.2 shows an example of what this could look like.

In Figure 10.2, the receiving party (the vice president) has previously described the inputs needed for the integration event to Marketing, Engineering, Purchasing, Accounting, Finance, and Sales. These departments will flow work within their own value streams in order to provide the vice president with the information needed at the integration event to create a product launch proposal. The vice president also has described the final deliverable required from each department, which in this case is a folder that will be placed into a three-ring binder at the integration event to make up the proposal.

Helpful Hint

If an integration event takes place and there are questions, clarifications, redesigning or overprocessing of information, or decisions, then it isn't a true integration event.

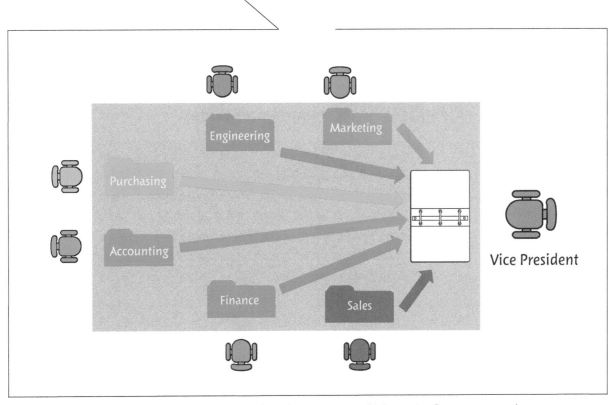

Figure 10.2 **An example of an integration event, where large amounts of information flow one way and are captured by the vice president in a three-ring binder.**

As each department completes its work to prepare the information needed for the integration event, they capture knowledge in terms of which parameters had to be negotiated with the vice president and which ones were okay as originally provided. This knowledge can then be used for future integration events to eliminate or minimize future negotiation.

At the time of the integration event, the vice president enters the conference room with the empty binder into which each department will place its folder. A representative from each department arrives with a folder (the required input) and places it into the binder to make up the product launch proposal (the required output). The vice president quickly reviews the files provided by each party to make sure everything required is present. Once confirmed, the integration event is over and everyone can leave the conference room.

There is no negotiating, bargaining, direction setting, or decision making during the integration event. The inputs required by the vice president to make up the product launch proposal were provided by each department at the time and place specified by the integration event.

After the integration event has concluded, the vice president processes the work resulting from the integration event on a fixed or triggered workflow cycle and then moves the information to another area of the company to continue the flow of information.

practical application **Human Resources Integration Events**

A review of the *Technical New Hire* value stream does not reveal any processes that occur infrequently or on a one-time basis. There are no large amounts of information that need to move from one area to another, nor is there a major handoff of information within the value stream. Therefore, look where the information goes after the completion of the last process. A review of the service family matrix created earlier will help do this (Figure 10.3).

	Collect Specifications for New Hire	Submit Formal Request	Candidate Search	Contact Recruiter	Review Resume	First Interview	Evaluate Prior Research	Technical Test 1	Technical Test 2	Technical Test 3	Evaluate Test Results	Review First Interview Results	Second Interview	Review Second Interview Results	Vice President Interview	Review VP Interview Results	C-Suite Interview	Review C-Suite Interview Results	Final Interview	Review Final Interview Results	Configure Compensation Pckg.	Create Offer Letter	Schedule Orientation
Managers	X	X	X		X	X						X	X	X	X	X			X	X	X	X	X
Engineers	X	X	X		X	X		X			X	X	X	X					X	X	X	X	X
R&D	X	X	X	X	X	X	X	X	X	X	X	X	X	X					X	X	X	X	X
Senior Execs.	X	X	X		X	X						X	X	X	X	X	X	X	X	X	X	X	X
IT	X	X	X		X	X		X	X		X	X	X	X					X·	X	X	X	X

Figure 10.3 **The original service family matrix created for the engineering and IT new hire service family.**

Once a candidate has been selected, Human Resources has a large quantity of information that needs to go to the start of another flow *(New Hire Orientation)*. A service family matrix for the *New Hire Orientation* value stream could be developed to determine the different services provided in orienting a new hire. The nine design guidelines would need to be applied to each value stream within *New Hire Orientation*, but these value steams could not begin processing their work until the *Technical New Hire* flow has been completed and the information passed along.

Given that there will be a large amount of information handed off to another value stream, this is a good place for an integration event. An integration event can be used here by matching the outputs of the *Technical New Hire* flow with the inputs of the *New Hire Orientation* flow. The outputs supplied by the *Technical New Hire* value stream could be put into a checklist form to ensure all of the information required is being provided along with the format in which it needs to be.

Knowledge relating to each candidate should be captured, ensuring the business has a formal record of the package that was offered to them and more. In this case, it will be important to capture the candidate's résumé, interview notes, starting salary, benefits, any negotiated terms, and other information most likely from the interviews or contained in the offer letter.

Other information can be captured as well. Understanding why an offer was rejected can help us understand more about the market conditions and what is needed to attract talented help. The details of how terms were negotiated (the initial offer versus any other offers) may help us understand our offer in the context of our market and competition. Once captured, all of this information, both the information that was used and the information that was not, can be formally entered into our HR database for further use, allowing us to improve our new hire process in the future.

practical application Engineering Integration Events

Similar to the *Technical New Hire value* stream, a review of the *Moderate Customer Redesign* value stream does not reveal any processes that occur infrequently or on a one-time basis. Within the value stream, there are no large amounts of information that need to move from one area to another, nor is there a major handoff of information within the value stream. Therefore, we would look to where the information goes after the completion of the last process.

A review of the service family matrix created earlier for *Moderate Customer Redesigns* will help us understand how this value stream is connected to the next process (Figure 10.4).

	Receive Request	Log Request in Database	Preliminary Design	Log Preliminary Drawing	Materials Verification	Preliminary Design Review	Final Design	Final Design Review	FMEA	Log / Update Final Drawing	Cost Analysis	Certify Design	Eng. Manager Sign-Off	Finance Sign-Off	General Manager Sign-Off	Upload to Operations DB	**Total**
Moderate	10	10	60	20	35	60	60	60	90	10	60	75	5	5	5	15	**580**

Figure 10.4 **The original service family matrix for *Moderate Customer Redesigns.***

An integration event would be useful at the end of the flow where *Moderate Customer Redesigns* are uploaded to the Operations database. Once the designs are uploaded, manufacturing and operations begin their part in producing the new customer redesign. Depending upon the application, the information provided by Engineering could only be one part of the entire package needed. After sign-off, an integration event could be held to combine all of the information, after which it would be uploaded to a database with other information as well. If the engineering work is all that is required and there is no need to combine it with other information, then we could upload the data as part of this value stream, because an integration event would not be needed.

In this case, Engineering provides a significant amount of the information needed and it does not need to be combined with other information. Therefore, we will leave the "Upload to Operations DB" process as part of this value stream and not use an integration event.

Action Item

· ·

Create integration events where necessary. Revisit the service family matrix to determine if an integration event can be used to connect this value stream with one either upstream or downstream.

Check off each step as it is completed.

☐ Create an integration event where necessary for the service family by reviewing the service family matrix and seeing if this value stream can be connected to another one either upstream or downstream.

☐ Determine the necessary input(s) required by the receiving party for the integration event.

☐ Determine the necessary output(s) of the providing parties for the integration event.

☐ Determine the timing of the integration event, when the work will flow, and when the integration event will be completed.

Acid Test

· ·

No discussion is occurring at the integration event. Employees are simply coming together to pull work forward, matching their outputs to the inputs required by the receiving party.

Action Item
Create an Integration Event

Name of the integration event

_____

_____

Sending Party   Receiving Party

_____

_____

_____ $\longrightarrow$

_____   _____

_____

_____

Information being transferred

_____

_____

Format of information being transferred

    File Type: Word _____   Excel _____   Other _____

    File Form: Electronic _____   Printed _____   Database Entry _____

Knowledge being captured

    Trade-Off Curve _____   A3 _____

    Cost Data Analysis _____   Other _____

Timing for the integration event

_____

_____

Location of the integration event

_____

_____

chapter
eleven

Guideline #6: Standard Work

Standard work ensures that flow in the office is repeatable and predictable, no matter who performs the work. Standard work also should put the knowledge captured into action and allow for the application of future captured knowledge. There are two levels of standard work: the *activity level* and the *flow level*.

Activity Level Standard Work

Standard work at the activity level is created by identifying the work content, tools, systems, forms, other information needed, and sequence required to complete the work. Once these are identified, a team approach can be used to set the best method. It's also important that all tools and materials required—reference databases and materials,

books, software (and software version), and sources of information—should be at the fingertips of the person performing the work. No searching for information or tools should be necessary.

Standard work at the activity level also should use photos with annotations for quick reference to allow an easy way to ensure everyone involved performs the tasks at a process in the same manner.

Standard work is needed for all the activities that happen within the processing cells and other standalone processes (Figure 11.1).

The goal of activity level standard work should be to create something (a document, spreadsheet, computer file, etc.) that can be given to someone who

Definition

 Activity level standard work is the documentation of the best method for performing each task that occurs at each process. It is the standard work for someone at his/her desk or workstation performing the work.

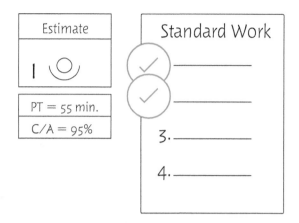

Figure 11.1 **Standard work at the activity level can use checklists.**

has never worked in the organization and, providing he or she has the requisite background in the required field, have the activity level standard work alone be enough to instruct him/her on how to do a particular job. This means that this person would be able to complete the required job and not need to ask any questions or resolve any ambiguities once he/she has the standard work document in hand. Ideally, the standard work document would be entirely visual in nature, or as visual as possible.

Over time, the person performing the job might not need to consult the standard work document every time he or she begins to work. However, in the beginning, it is a good idea to follow the steps to ensure good habits are developed. Also, the same document can be used to cross-train other employees on different jobs. It might not be possible to fully cross-train people if the background or requirements for a certain job (like its core work) require too much specialization, but more cross-training means more opportunity to move around work elements when balancing employees' work to create part-time processing cells.

Helpful Hint

To help construct activity level standard work and zero in on the appropriate level of detail required, think of what a new employee who has never worked in the company before would need to know in order to complete a particular job. This will ensure that the activity level standard work is comprehensive and provides the necessary level of detail required.

Flow Level Standard Work

For flow level standard work, the goal is for everyone in the value stream flow to answer the following five questions:

1. How do I know what to work on next?

2. Where do I get my work from?

3. How long should it take me to perform my work?

4. Where do I send my work?

5. When I send my work, is flow still normal?

The answers to these questions will allow work to flow between processes and processing cells without chasing information, seeking out supervisors, holding status meetings, or needing to ask questions.

In Figure 11.2, flow level standard work would need to exist at the FIFO (first in, first out) lanes before and after any process or processing cell.

Definition

 Flow level standard work describes how each process is connected to the next process, what path information will follow, how much work that path will hold under normal flow conditions, and when the work should move along that path.

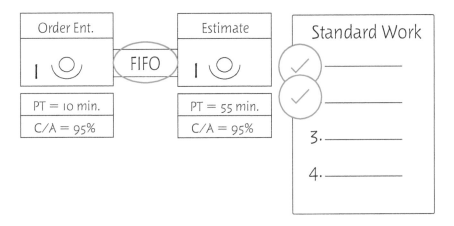

Figure 11.2 **Flow level standard work would need to exist at the FIFO lane that connects these two processes.**

Helpful Hint

The five questions for flow should not be answered with: "I look at a schedule." The activity and flow level standard work should be able to answer the five questions for flow on their own.

In general, flow level standard work will be covered by the rules that govern how FIFO lanes and workflow cycles function. For example, if there is no work pending for a workflow cycle, then there is no need for everyone to show up and the time should be used for other work. Therefore, the standard work might include appointing someone (who can see the FIFO lane feeding the workflow cycle) to send an email or text message an hour beforehand stating that the workflow cycle for a particular service family is not needed on that day.

Having good standard work at the activity level and the flow level is key to successfully sustaining value stream flow. When something goes wrong and the information is not flowing as designed, we should check the standard work to see if it is correct and still being used.

practical application ## Human Resources Standard Work

There are two types of standard work: the activity level and the flow level. Both will need to be considered for the *Technical New Hire* service family and will need to be created at each process or part-time processing cell (activity level standard work) and the connections between them (flow level standard work).

Activity Level Standard Work for *Technical New Hires*

For the *Technical New Hire* service family, we would need to develop a standard work document or form for the review of each applicant's interview results, or at least for certain parts of the interview. Different criteria could be established, perhaps problem-solving ability, communication and explanation skills, design capability, and more. These fields could then be graded 1 to 10, with standard work on how to grade each applicant. The reviewers could then use this document as a jumping off point when they evaluate candidates. While this might not be able to capture everything a candidate has to offer, it can help standardize part of the review process.

Helpful Hint

Documenting how a specific workflow cycle will work, how often it will run, when it will run, and how much work it will perform is a good way to create flow level standard work.

Flow Level Standard Work for *Technical New Hires*

When it comes to flow level standard work for this service family, the connections between each process need to be considered, which, in this case, are FIFO lanes (and usually will be in other cases as well). By this point in the flow design, some basic flow level standard work will have been established just from the FIFO lanes and workflow cycles that have been created. These have their own rules about when work is to be withdrawn for processing and the sequence in which it will happen.

However, this alone will not be sufficient flow level standard work (Figure 11.3).

At the "Evaluate Test Results" process, flow level standard work will need to be created that governs how to withdraw work from which multiple FIFO lane, in what quantity, and when, if both candidate types are being processed at the same time. This shouldn't be too difficult; we would just need to set a rule, such as IT candidates should be processed first if there is a choice.

practical application Engineering **Standard Work**

When it comes to activity level standard work in Engineering, much of what was just covered in the previous section on Human Resources holds true for Engineering as well. Typically, Engineering has rigorous standards to which it must adhere when designing new products, and these should be part of the standard work. Referencing standard designs, approved vendors, and, most importantly, previously captured knowledge are important components of the standard work for Engineering.

💬

Helpful Hint

A completed future state map that has applied all nine guidelines in this book is a good way to document flow level standard work. A good way to show the standard work in action at the flow level is to have visuals throughout the office that show how processes are connected along with how much work should be between each process at any given time.

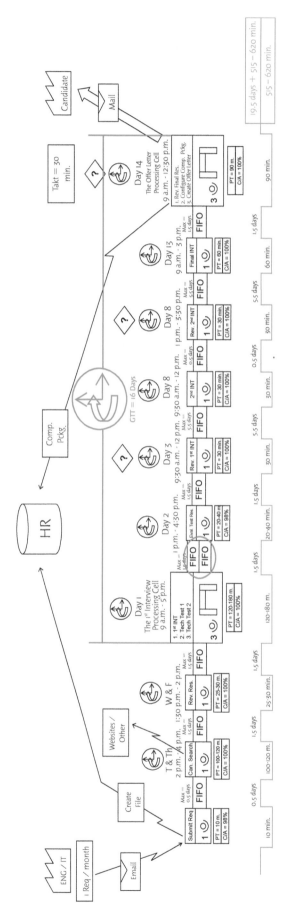

Figure 11.3 The flow for the *Technical New Hire* service family.

Activity Level Standard Work for *Moderate Customer Redesigns*

The main difference in activity level standard work with Engineering is that parts of it will be difficult to completely standardize. Certain tasks that Engineering performs *will* be capable of standardization, but perhaps not all of them.

When designs come in, an engineer might not know where to begin until the design is in front of him. However, the engineer will likely use the same *process* on the current design as he will on every other design that comes across his desk, and this process is what should be focused on when creating activity level standard work for the design activities in Engineering. While it might not be possible to standardize every design, effort should be made to standardize the *approach* that is taken to every design.

Engineers might instinctively do this already on their own, but it's still a good idea to try to formally standardize the approach, because engineering staff will end up learning from one another during this process and a better overall approach will likely be determined if everyone works on it together.

Also, similar to what was talked about in the HR section with regard to cross-training, standardizing the approach that engineers take to *Moderate Customer Redesigns* will make cross-training other engineering employees easier than it would otherwise be and also will help orient new employees more quickly. It will help new employees contribute to the organization faster as well.

Flow Level Standard Work for *Moderate Customer Redesigns*

Creating flow level standard work for the design portions of the *Moderate Customer Redesign* flow will be similar to creating flow level standard work in the *Technical New Hire* value stream. Workflow cycles have been created for each process or part-time processing cell and also for logging drawings, materials verification, and updating the Operations database.

Flow level standard work will need to be created that governs when each FIFO lane will be emptied. Much of this will be determined by the workflow cycle that exists for the specific process or part-time processing cell in question, but additional flexibility can be built into the system of flow by setting thresholds at some of the FIFO lanes to help the system adjust to different mixes of *Customer Redesigns* that may come into the business.

For example, setting thresholds for the FIFO lanes that connect "Preliminary Design" to each of the next processes in the three different *Customer Redesign* service families could help inform engineers where their resources are needed on a particular day if the mix in demand has shifted.

At the beginning of the day, someone from Engineering might check the FIFO lanes for *Standard, Moderate,* and *Complex Customer Redesigns.* If each FIFO lane is below a certain threshold, they might be processed normally with the established workflow cycles. However, if one of the FIFO lanes is beyond its established threshold, then the workflow cycles could be adjusted to account for the fact that more of one particular type of *Customer Redesign* has come into the business than originally anticipated. Standard work would need to be developed around how the workflow cycles are adjusted, otherwise we will be relying on management decision making.

If more *Moderate Customer Redesigns* are received than are expected, the workflow cycles for them could be run longer or more frequently for that day or even over the course of the week. This will enable the Engineering department to keep up with the shifting mix of customer demand *while still working within the rules of flow.*

This last point is very important and will be covered in much more detail in Chapter 14 (Guideline #9) on dealing with changes in demand. The previous solution of running workflow cycles longer did not involve seeking out managers or supervisors to determine what to do if the FIFO thresholds were exceeded. Rather, this was built into the flow level standard work for how the connections will operate between the processes.

Because the process times for the three different types of *Customer Redesigns* vary so drastically, some thought would have to be put into determining where these FIFO thresholds should be and what kind of response they should mandate, because having more *Complex Customer Redesigns* than expected will entail significantly more time to work through than having more *Standard Customer Redesigns.*

Action Item

· ·

Create activity level standard work for the processes and processing cells in the value stream. Create flow level standard work for the FIFO lanes that connect the processes and processing cells in the value stream. Also, create flow level standard work for the workflow cycles at each process and processing cell.

Check off each step as it is completed.

☐ Determine the best method for completing each activity in the service family. Take into account the work content, tools, systems, forms, other information needed, and sequence required to complete the work.

☐ Standardize the procedure for the completion of each activity using a team approach.

☐ Write up, document, and distribute the established activity level standard work.

☐ Create flow level standard work for the connections between the processes and processing cells. Make sure the five key questions for value stream flow in the office can be answered.

☐ Create standard work for the capturing of knowledge at the end of each workflow cycle and integration event.

Acid Test

· ·

Someone from another department can use the activity level standard work to complete all nonspecialized tasks, such as operating computer systems, locating files, and so on. Someone from another department is able to follow the flow from process to process using only the flow level standard work provided.

Action Item
Create Activity Level Standard Work

Name of processes or cells

_____

_____

_____

Work content

_____

_____

_____

Required sequence of completion

_____

_____

_____

Tools and materials required

_____

_____

_____

Systems needed

_____

_____

_____

Forms or other information needed

_____

_____

_____

Notes

_____

_____

_____

Action Item
Create Flow Level Standard Work

Name of processes or cells connected

_____
_____
_____

How do I know what to work on next?

_____
_____
_____

Where do I get my work from?

_____
_____
_____

How long should it take me to perform my work?

_____
_____
_____

Where do I send my work?

_____
_____
_____

When I send my work, is flow still normal?

_____
_____
_____

Notes

_____
_____
_____

chapter
twelve

Guideline #7: Single-Point Initialization

One of the keys to achieving flow and guaranteed turnaround times lies in eliminating the constant reprioritization of work, which is often based on personal preferences or local management changing priorities to try and optimize their respective areas.

Constant reprioritization of work is detrimental to flow. When each employee looks at the work waiting to be done and picks and chooses what he/she will work on next according to his/her own priorities or understanding of business priorities, it is impossible to guarantee turnaround times through the value stream or create a predictable flow of work. The randomness in selecting what to work on next at each activity makes lead times and response times to customers or other areas of the company unpredictable and causes management to become involved. In order to

maintain flow and establish guaranteed turnaround times, this randomness in selecting what to work on next needs to be eliminated .

To eliminate the randomness in selecting work, we would *try* to set one single point within the value stream at which work is introduced from outside the value stream by the customer. This sequence would then be preserved and continued all the way through the flow to the customer through continuous flow processing cells or FIFO (first in, first out) connections.

However, even with closely defined service families and dedicated resources to work in them, it's often difficult to create a flow where work is initialized at one process and then maintained in a fixed sequence from this point to delivery. Therefore, it's important in

Definition

The **initialization point** for the value stream is the one process or processing cell at which work is introduced into the flow from outside the value stream. This is the first point in the value stream at which the sequence of work is established and should be set as far upstream as possible.

Definition

Sequencing points are designated processes or processing cells in the value stream at which work can be resequenced due to external factors.

the office that we address this by having a single point where the work gets initialized into the value stream, but that we also allow for points in the flow where work can be resequenced due to external factors.

Setting the Initialization Point

There should be only one initialization point for each value stream. Ideally, we want to set the initialization point where the request first comes into the value stream from the customer. The initialization point should be positioned all the way upstream. If this is not possible, then it should be as close as possible to the first activity in the value stream. If we are able to set the initialization point at the first process, then each process and processing cell that follows can be connected with either continuous flow or FIFO from the beginning of the value stream all the way to its end. These connections preserve the initial sequence of work created at the initialization point, as the rules of continuous flow and FIFO do not allow work to be reshuffled or reprioritized, and help maintain the GTT through the value stream.

The key with setting an initialization point is establishing rules or guidelines on how work will enter the value stream. These guidelines determine the sequence based on business needs, the simplest being "first in, first out" no matter who the customer is. However, each business can determine additional guidelines based on other factors, such as customer, order size, potential for future work, customer-requested turnaround time, importance to the business, and so on. It is important that standard work be developed for how the sequencing occurs prior to work entering the value stream. This could be presented in a flow chart or logic chart used by the person who sets the sequence. It could be a simple rule like always take the new work first, or it may be a more complex set of rules to follow that allow certain customers, kinds of jobs, or kinds of problems to take priority. Again, the sequence should be set without the need for management.

In Figure 12.1, the initialization point for this value stream is at the first process, "Order Entry." The initialization point is depicted as a red arrow over the process that is serving as the initialization point.

Helpful Hint

The initialization point is also a good place to check the quality of inputs. Incoming work can be checked according to standard work and should only be allowed into the value stream if it adheres to the standard work. Otherwise, constant rework will prevent the value stream from achieving the guaranteed turnaround time to the customer.

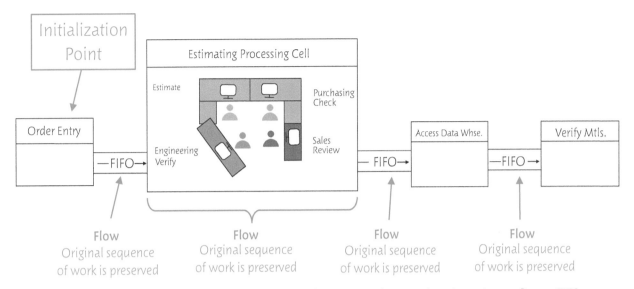

Figure 12.1 **The "Order Entry" process can serve as the initialization point because there is continuous flow or FIFO from this point forward.**

Determining Additional Sequencing Points

While ideally we would like to fix the sequence of work at the initialization point and then never have to alter it again, external factors sometimes prohibit this from being possible. Often, there are points where work leaves the value stream and then must return later on, or work can be impacted by some other external factor that unavoidably influences the sequence of work.

There will only be one initialization point in each value stream, but there might be additional sequencing points after the initialization point. Sequencing points are not places where we allow new work to enter the value stream. Work might be *re*-entering the value stream from an outside source, but it will already have been placed into the value stream at the initialization point.

Helpful Hint

The need for additional sequencing points within a value stream is determined by external factors, not management priorities. For example, if work leaves the value stream for vendor review in FIFO sequence, but returns at different times and out of order, then it may be resequenced as needed as it comes back into the value stream.

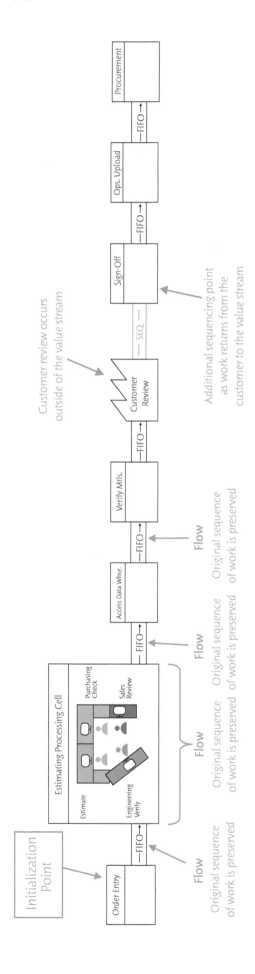

Figure 12.2 The "Sign-Off" process would be a sequencing point, because work is returning to the value stream from an external customer review.

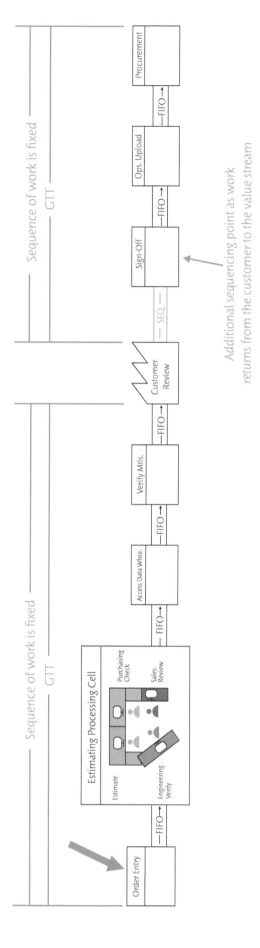

Figure 12.3 Sequencing points create blocks of flow in the value stream within which the sequence of work is fixed. The sequence of work from "Order Entry" to the FIFO lane feeding "Customer Review" is fixed, and the sequence of work from the FIFO lane feeding "Sign-Off" to "Procurement" is fixed as well. The two sequences of work could be different, however, because work can be reshuffled at the sequencing point of "Sign-Off." Within each block of flow, the GTT is fixed.

Figure 12.2 shows a continuation of the value stream seen in Figure 12.1. Work must leave the value stream after "Verify Materials" to undergo a customer review that is external to the value stream. Therefore, the "Sign-Off" process can be a sequencing point. When work reenters the value stream at this process, it can be resequenced according to predefined standard work before being placed into the FIFO lane. We note the sequencing point on a value stream map by writing "SEQ" (for "sequence") in the FIFO lane before the process or cell designated as a sequencing point.

By establishing sequencing points within the value stream, we fix sections of the value stream in which the sequence of work cannot be changed. Within these blocks, work is locked into a fixed sequence and the turnaround time is guaranteed. In Figure 12.3, there are two separate sections of value stream flow within which the sequence of work remains fixed. The sequence in one section might be different from the sequence in the other, but once fixed within a section, it would not change, thus preserving the GTT within each section of the flow.

Human Resources
Single-Point Initialization

To determine the initialization point in the *Technical New Hire* service family, start at the beginning of the value stream and locate where the work is introduced into the value stream. This is the first process, "Submit Request." The sequence of work will be initially fixed at "Submit Request" (Figure 12.4). Note that this is not where the GTT begins because the next two processes are research oriented, and not every candidate makes it in for an interview.

Helpful Hint

Having good activity and flow level standard work will help ensure the GTT (guaranteed turnaround time) is maintained after the initialization point. The goal is for the initialization point to trigger the start of the GTT, and without robust standard work at each process and the connections between them, this will be difficult to achieve.

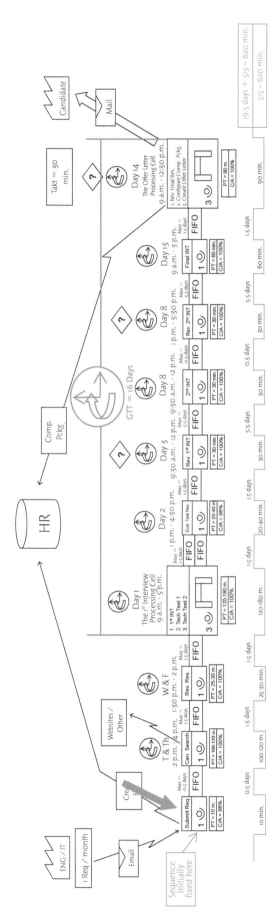

Figure 12.4 **The initialization point occurs at "Submit Request."**

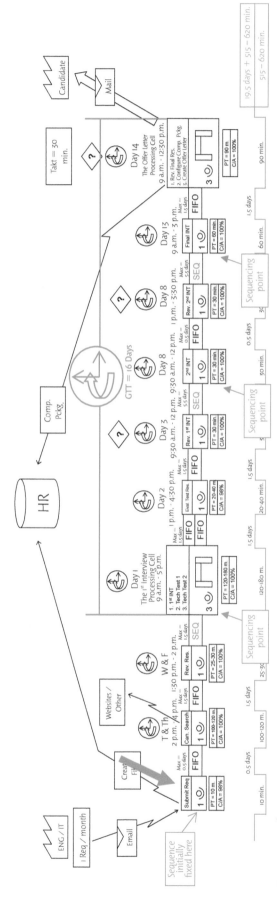

Figure 12.5 **Three more sequencing points are needed: at the First Interview Processing Cell, "Second Interview," and "Final Interview." Setting up the three interviews will depend on candidates' availability.**

After the initialization point, there are three more points in the value stream at which the flow depends on a response from someone outside of the value stream. These natural breaks in flow are based on candidates' availability to come in for their first, second, and final interviews. Therefore, we can set three sequencing points in the value stream: at the First Interview Processing Cell, "Second Interview," and "Final Interview" (Figure 12.5).

practical application | Engineering
Single-Point Initialization

In the *Moderate Customer Redesign* service family, the initialization point would be the first process, "Receive/Log Req in Database." After "Preliminary Design" has finished its work and determined what types of *Customer Redesigns* have come into the business, it might be necessary to resequence any *Moderate Customer Redesigns* based on the needs of the business.

The external factor in play here that necessitates the sequencing point is that there is no way of knowing what type of *Customer Redesign* has been requested from the business until "Preliminary Design" finishes its work. Because of this, we will set a sequencing point at "Log Preliminary Drawing" and allow the sequence of work to be reshuffled in the FIFO lane before this process (Figure 12.6).

Helpful Hint

We want there to be as few sequencing points as possible in the value stream. The more sequencing points there are, the more opportunities there are to potentially disrupt the guaranteed turnaround time for the overall flow.

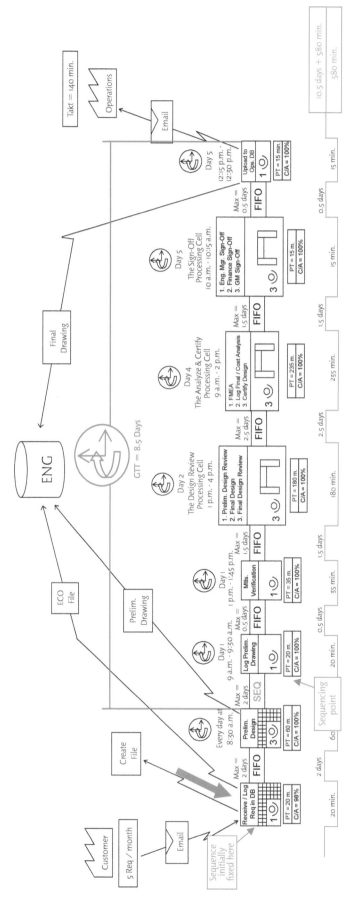

Figure 12.6 The initialization point for the *Moderate Customer Redesign* family is at "Receive/Log Req in Database" and there is a sequencing point at "Log Preliminary Drawing."

Action Item
. . . .

Create an initialization point for the value stream. Determine if there are any other processes at which work would need to be resequenced due to external factors. Create standard work for how to sequence work at these sequencing points.

Check off each step as it is completed.

☐ Determine which process in the flow will be the initialization point.

☐ Create standard work for how the sequence of work will be determined and set at the initialization point.

☐ Using continuous flow and FIFO, determine how the sequence of work will be set and preserved once it leaves the initialization point. How will each employee know what to work on next?

☐ Determine if any other processes will need to serve as additional sequencing points due to external factors.

☐ Create standard work for how the sequence of work will be determined and set at each additional sequencing point.

Acid Test
. . . .

Someone from another department can tell how each process after the initialization point knows what to work on next and what standard work is used to determine the sequence of work at the initialization point and any additional sequencing points. Note that if flow exists from the initialization point all the way to the customer, the answers should not include asking questions or seeking out supervisors.

Action Item
Create Single-Point Initialization

Process or cell that will serve as the initialization point

_____
_____
_____

What standard work will be used to determine the sequence of work at the initialization point?

_____
_____
_____

Additional sequencing points required

_____
_____
_____

External factors necessitating additional sequencing points

_____
_____
_____

What standard work will be used to determine the sequence of work at the additional sequencing points?

_____
_____
_____

Notes

_____
_____
_____

chapter thirteen

Guideline #8: Pitch

While the previous guidelines were all about designing flow, pitch is a tool that enables anyone to easily see whether the flow is operating normally without having to interrupt or ask questions of employees. Even a visitor to your business should be able to tell if the flow is on time to customer demand using pitch.

Pitch is checked at predetermined times and points in the value stream and indicates whether work is flowing on time to customer demand. Pitch should be checked at a meaningful point in the value stream, the idea being that if output at this process is on time, then the entire value stream should be on time to customer demand. For example, suppose a processing cell near the end of the value stream should produce five quotes per hour. If, in fact, it does produce five quotes per hour throughout its workflow

cycle, then it's safe to say it is on time and is being fed enough work, which means the processes upstream are also on time.

In Figure 13.1, pitch is at the workflow cycle for this processing cell. A green flag is used to indicate that the work in the flow has been completed on time, and a red flag to indicate work is behind.

Keep in mind that pitch can still be checked, even if there are no processing cells in the flow for the service family. A good place for this is at the end of a workflow cycle, whenever and wherever that is. If pitch is checked at the completion of each workflow cycle, then the team knows the workflow cycles are operating as they should. Therefore, the work is flowing as designed. A green flag would be raised at

Definition

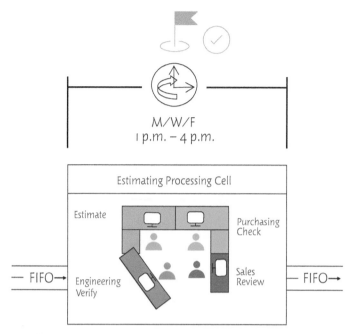

Pitch is a preset time-frame that lets everyone who works in the flow know, in a visual manner, whether the flow is on time.

Figure 13.1 **The processing cell and workflow cycle created for it represent a good opportunity to use pitch to identify whether the flow is on time or behind.**

the end of each workflow cycle if it was completed on time and the FIFO lane feeding it successfully emptied, or if the workflow cycle achieved the appropriate output. The system of red and green flags could be used here as well (Figure 13.2).

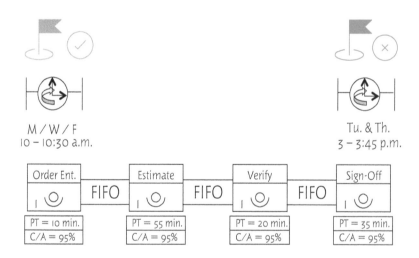

Figure 13.2 **Pitch could be created at the end of workflow cycles, even when there aren't any processing cells. The "Order Entry" workflow cycle was on time; the "Sign-Off" workflow cycle was not on time.**

Helpful Hint

It is important that pitch is visual so everyone in the organization can see it. A simple "flag" on a cubical wall or desk can indicate if pitch was made or missed.

Four Attributes of a Good Pitch

While there are many ways to create pitch, a good pitch in the office has four key attributes. Pitch should be visual, physical, binary, and anticipated:

1. **Visual**

    People should be able to see the pitch signal as they walk through the office because it's happening. It shouldn't be hidden away in a spreadsheet or online dashboard that has to be opened and checked.

2. **Physical**

    The best time to check pitch is when a physical activity happens, e.g., someone shows up at the end of each workflow cycle to physically take the information. If information is flowing digitally, think about a physical signal that has to be moved, such as raising a green flag.

3. **Binary**

    This means that the pitch was either met or not met. The flow is either on time or it isn't. There is no "almost on time."

4. **Anticipated**

    Similar to trains arriving at preset times to move people, pitch happens at preset times. Everyone in the office will know when the "information train" (or pitch) will occur, meaning they can self-check their progress according to this schedule.

Given the digital realities of the modern office, creating pitch might seem impractical. However, don't let this hinder the creation of physical and visual pitch. Remind people of the power of taking digital work and making it physical and visual. If work is completed on a computer, pitch can be shown using a flag system or a big green or red magnet on the side of a cubicle. It could even be linked to a FIFO lane, such as: if the flow is on time, then this FIFO lane should be emptied by noon.

Helpful Hint

Pitch should not be determined in a status meeting. In fact, you may find that status meetings are no longer needed with the implementation of these guidelines.

There are many other ways to adopt the guideline of pitch. We have seen teams use flags, dart boards, Lego® pieces, and many other creative solutions to measure and show pitch, even though the work is digital. In fact, we often use smartphone apps that push pitch status alerts to team members. Remember that good pitch is visual, physical, binary, and anticipated, so encourage your team to be creative.

practical application | Human Resources Pitch

In the *Technical New Hire* value stream, pitch could theoretically happen anywhere, but it should happen at least at the initialization point, each processing cell, and the three sequencing points (Figure 13.3).

To create pitch, some sort of visual signal would be needed, perhaps a green flag if work was completed on time and a red flag if it was not. There are virtually endless options here. Some companies set up a target and "shoot it" with a toy gun that fires foam darts with suction cups, thus sticking to the target as an identifier for when pitch has been met. If the right number of darts is not present on the target (at the dedicated time), then everyone knows pitch has been missed and the workflow cycle did not complete its work on time.

The *Technical New Hire* value stream will need to have robust activity level standard work, and employees should be able to determine where they are and where they should be (based on the takt established) in the workflow cycle at all times.

If they are halfway through the Offer Letter Processing Cell and realize they are behind and won't catch up, then a red flag is displayed outside of the conference room where the processing cell takes place, and this lets everyone know that the flow is behind. Reacting in this way allows the flow to be corrected before the GTT (guaranteed turnaround time) is missed and the mailing of the offer letter to the selected candidate is delayed. This would be done by running the workflow cycle a little longer and having another employee fill out information on the offer letter that is not proprietary or confidential to the candidate.

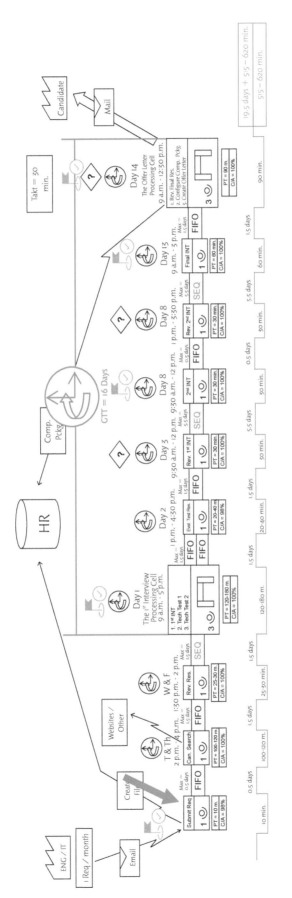

Figure 13.3 **The pitch created for the *Technical New Hire* service family.**

For the *Moderate Customer Redesign* flow, pitch will be checked at the initialization point ("Receive/Log Req in Database"), the sequencing point ("Log Preliminary Design"), and the final process in the value stream ("Upload to Ops. DB"). We will create pitch at the final process in the value stream in order to check if the end-to-end flow has been completed on time. We will also create pitch at "Preliminary Design," since this is the process at which we determine the type of *Customer Redesign* that has come into the business (Figure 13.4).

Similar to HR, there would need to be a visual indicator that pitch has been attained at each processing cell, and this could be done in any number of ways. While a green flag is used at the conclusion of each processing cell to signal that pitch has been attained, this information is also shown on display screens in common viewing areas around the organization and colored green on the screen (or red if pitch has not been attained), thus enabling everyone in the organization to see if the processing cells are on time or behind (Figure 13.5).

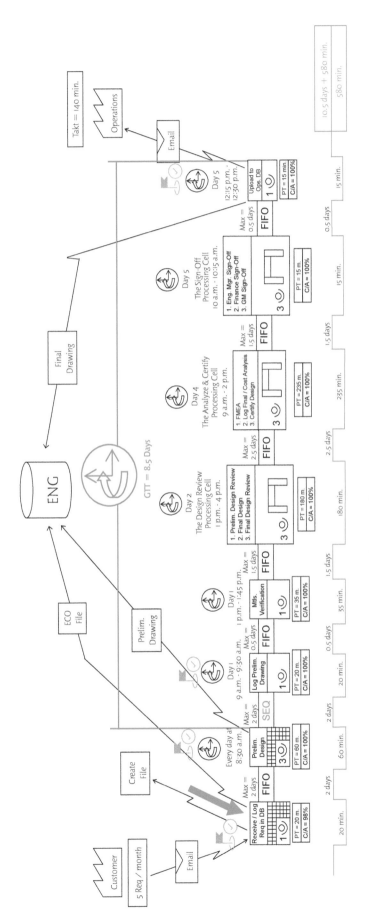

Figure 13.4 **The pitch created for the *Moderate Customer Redesign* family.**

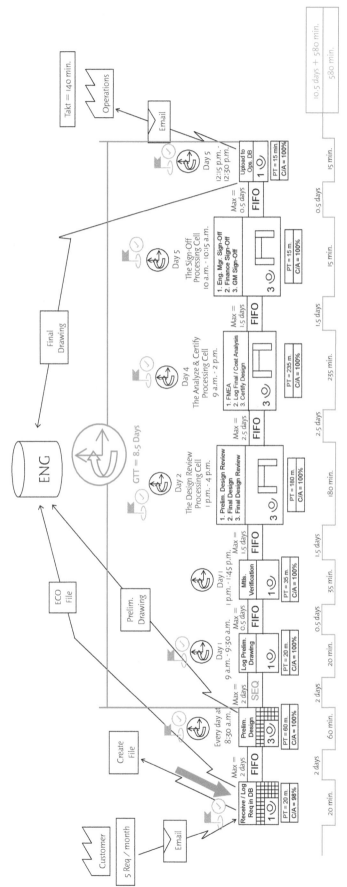

Figure 13.5 Pitch is created at each processing cell at the end of its workflow cycle. A physical green flag is displayed if pitch has been attained, and this information also is displayed on plasma screens around the company and colored green (or red if pitch is missed).

Action Item

Create pitch for any processing cells created, or for workflow cycles if there aren't any processing cells.

Check off each step as it is completed.

☐ Determine where pitch should be created.

☐ Determine how often or when pitch should be checked.

☐ Determine how each pitch mechanism will meet the four attributes of pitch.

☐ Determine how pitch will function for processes, processing cells, or work that is mostly digital in nature.

Acid Test

Someone from another department can tell if the team is on time to customer demand just by looking.

Action Item
Create Pitch

Processes or cells where pitch will be created

_____
_____
_____

Frequency with which we will know if pitch has been attained

_____
_____
_____

Describe how the four attributes of pitch will be met

_____
_____
_____

Describe how the digital will be made physical where the pitch is mostly electronic in nature

_____
_____
_____

Notes

_____
_____
_____

chapter
fourteen

Guideline #9: Changes in Demand

Back when we first created takt capabilities, we defined a level of demand and mix of deliverables that the value stream would be capable of handling that would satisfy 80 percent of normal conditions. However, it is very common for the demand for a service family to fluctuate either above or below this established threshold (Figure 14.1).

Demand Fluctuations

When fluctuations in demand happen while operating under the normal takt capability, we need to examine the front end of the business and consider the orders coming in, inquiries being made, or inputs into the value stream. When examining and analyzing these factors, we must determine whether they are indicative of a temporary fluctuation in demand or a true, permanent increase (or decrease) in demand. If it turns out that we are experiencing a true, permanent change in customer demand, then

we need to switch to another takt capability and begin operating according to its activity and flow level standard work. The new takt capability must be preestablished, and it typically involves a complete end-to-end redesign of the value stream using the previous eight guidelines. Standard work also should be established for when to switch to the new takt capability.

An example of why we would need to switch to another takt capability could be because Engineering needs twice the normal number of designs, as more products than normal are being launched within a quarter. Another example would be Human Resources needing to hire three times the normal number of employees due to a recent acquisition. In these cases, we are able to recognize the underlying cause for switching takt capabilities and understand that the incidents prompting the switch are not temporary.

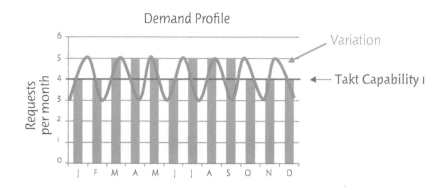

Figure 14.1 **Fluctuations above or below the established takt capability will happen.**

However, if we are unable to determine the cause of the demand fluctuation, then we should check to see if the market is trending upward. If it is, then we will need to switch takt capabilities to handle the increase in demand. If we cannot determine the cause and the market is not trending upward, then it is likely just a temporary fluctuation in demand that will not require a change in takt capability. Instead, it will be handled differently.

Changing Takt Capabilities

If customer demand changes permanently, then it's time to look at switching to another preestablished takt capability. When this happens, *preestablished* is the key word.

Figure 14.2 shows a jump in the demand for the service in June, which would mean switching takt capabilities to handle this increase in demand. We can determine this by looking at the front end of the business. Demand falls off in November, dictating a switch back to takt capability one.

The frequency with which a value stream should switch modes depends on the demand profile and the GTT (guaranteed turnaround time) required of the value stream. For longer lead time value streams, such as Engineering

Helpful Hint

If an inbound FIFO (first in, first out) stays in the red for a few days, it may be a good idea to find out if this is a real change from the process or value stream that is feeding the inbound FIFO or an overall change in demand. This could involve a conversation with another part of the company, the sales team, another front end part of the business, or perhaps even the customer. The idea here isn't to change how much work flows in, but rather to understand if the team needs to change takt capabilities to support the new change. The team should be the one making this happen, not management or the decisions of managers.

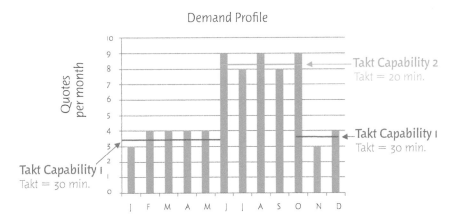

Figure 14.2 **A demand profile showing an increase in monthly demand and the new takt capability required to handle it.**

Change Orders, it may be okay to check which mode the team should be in each week and shift accordingly. However, when working on a higher volume, shorter lead time value stream, such as quoting, the shifts may occur daily. If the business needs a two-day GTT on quotes in order to stay competitive, the team may assess the inbound FIFO each morning to determine what mode they will need to work in that day in order to maintain the GTT.

In Figure 14.3, the demand changes enough from week to week that different takt capabilities are needed.

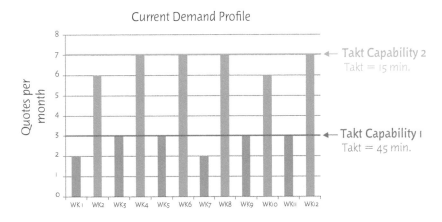

Figure 14.3 **It will be necessary to switch between takt capabilities each time demand changes from one mode to another.**

Helpful Hint

Be careful not to confuse a temporary fluctuation in demand with a permanent or long-lasting increase. A temporary fluctuation in demand will be absorbed by the FIFO lanes and will no longer be present in the value stream after a short amount of time.

Designing Different Takt Capabilities

Before new takt capabilities can be created, everyone must first understand how the designed future state value stream is intended to operate under the normal takt capability that satisfies 80 percent of normal conditions. Each additional takt capability must be designed ahead of time using the nine guidelines (even this guideline, #9) so we know how to recognize another change in demand that requires a change in takt capability.

There needs to be a standardized method for communicating a change in takt capability to everyone who works in the value stream so everyone understands the takt capability under which they are operating at all times. The person or team responsible for switching takt capabilities needs to be predefined as well. If possible, there should be standard work for determining when to switch takt capabilities.

Designing how the value stream will function under the new takt capability involves setting a new takt time to support it, the possibilities of adding parallel processing cells that perform work simultaneously, routing work to different resources using FIFO lanes, establishing new times for the workflow cycles to run, and creating a pitch that matches the new demand. We also might change the physical way in which work flows through the building.

One of the most important guidelines to consider when designing new takt capabilities is standard work, which might need to be altered for each process, processing cell, or process connection. If the existing standard work is robust and sufficient for the new takt capability, then it might allow us to bring in additional resources and train them quickly (and also ensure everyone is doing the work the same way). Having good standard work at the flow level allows us to understand how work will flow and what the timing of the flow will be and have visuals for flow preestablished for each takt capability.

Helpful Hint

If the workflow cycles change with a new takt capability, it could mean that the FIFO lanes associated with them need to be resized.

Ultimately, we want the effect of switching takt capabilities to be like flipping a light switch. Everyone should know exactly what to do when that switch is flipped and how work should flow through the office. This will make switching takt capabilities seamless and enable the business to respond quickly to true changes in customer demand (Figure 14.4).

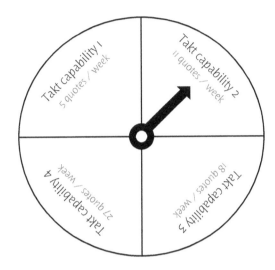

Figure 14.4 **Switching takt capability modes should be easy, like turning the pointer on a dial.**

Helpful Hint

A good way to handle an increase in demand without changing the physical design of the value stream is to run the processing cells and workflow cycles more often. In this manner, information will flow at a higher velocity through the same physical structure of the value stream.

Human Resources
Changes in Demand

The demand for the *Technical New Hire* service family will triple in May, so we will need to use the higher takt capability designed to handle this increase (Figure 14.5).

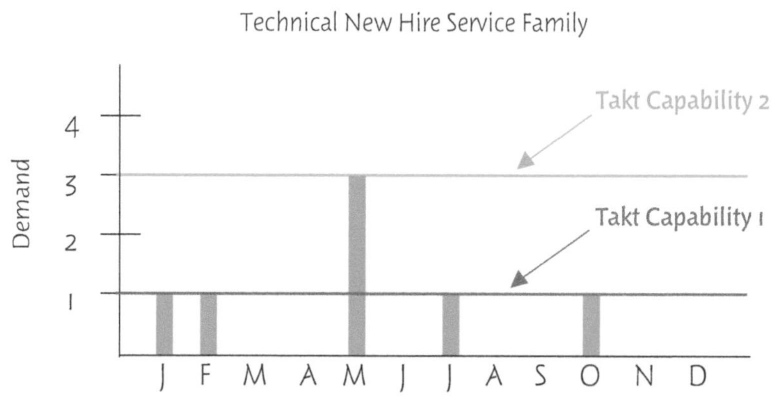

Technical New Hire Service Family

Figure 14.5 The demand profile for the *Technical New Hire* service family, showing the spike in demand in May.

There is a significant difference in the randomness of the demand for May compared with the other months. In the other months where candidates are hired, the business will not necessarily know when résumés will arrive, but because matriculating undergraduates are being targeted in May at a job fair, the business *will* know when it will receive candidates' résumés because there will be a hard deadline that the business can set. This enables the business to have more predictability around the input to the *Technical New Hire* value stream flow.

Therefore, instead of using triggered workflow cycles for this value stream, the enhanced predictability with which candidates will be identified will enable the business to use fixed workflow cycles instead. The process time of the "Candidate Search" and "Review Resume" activities will triple because there will be more new hires to process, but these activities can be completed *on the same day* because the business will know when candidates will hand in their résumés (Figure 14.6). The team will run the existing workflow cycles longer and run a little bit of overtime on the Monday during this peak demand month.

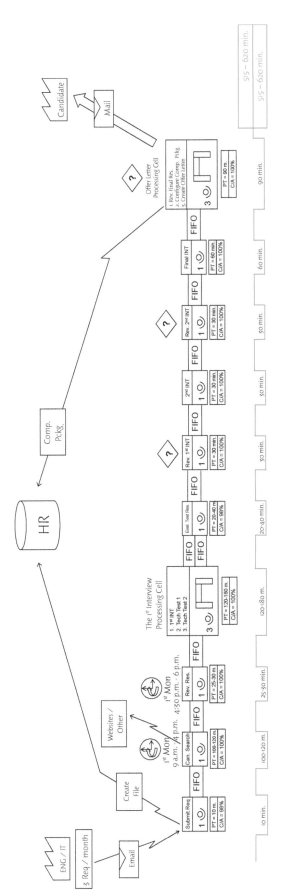

Figure 14.6 **The workflow cycles for the first two activities, working under the higher takt capability.**

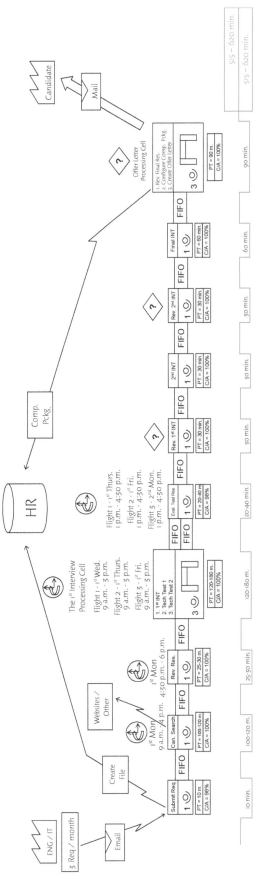

Figure 14.7 **The workflow cycles for the First Interview Processing Cell and "Evaluate Test Results."**

The business likes to interview five candidates for a position, so if the business is hiring three positions, then fifteen candidates will be interviewed in total, five candidates per "flight." Figure 14.7 shows what the workflow cycle will look like for the First Interview Processing Cell, as well as the workflow cycle for the "Evaluate Test Results" activity, for takt capability two. Standard work will need to be created for the multiple FIFO lanes that feed "Evaluate Test Results." All IT candidates will be processed first, then the engineering candidates will be processed.

For the next activity, "Review First Interview Results," all candidates from all flights would be reviewed at the same time, so the workflow cycle would have to run longer (Figure 14.8).

Scheduling the second interview will still take some time to coordinate, but once everyone has been called back a week later, all second interviews can take place on the same day, because it would take a total of seven and a half hours to complete. All the second interview results can be reviewed on the next day (Figure 14.9).

After another week to schedule the final interviews, they would need to be run over two days to have enough time to interview all of the candidates. The results could then all be reviewed on the next available day, and this day also would be when compensation packages are configured and offer letters mailed in the Offer Letter Processing Cell (Figure 14.10).

Sizing FIFO Lanes under Takt Capability Two

With the workflow cycles determined, the FIFO lanes can be sized. Similar to how we previously sized FIFO lanes, they must be sized to hold more than the minimum amount of work that would be dictated by the workflow cycles. If they fill up, we would not want the previous activities to stop working. However, we also might need to increase the size of a FIFO lane further with an extended zone to accommodate additional abnormal flow. This extended zone would be used if things go wrong beyond the level for which we have initially planned.

Figure 14.11 shows the FIFO sizes while operating under the higher takt capability. The FIFO lane connecting "Evaluate Test Results" with "Review First Interview Results" will need to hold three days worth of work because the first group of candidates finishes on Thursday but all the results are not reviewed until Tuesday.

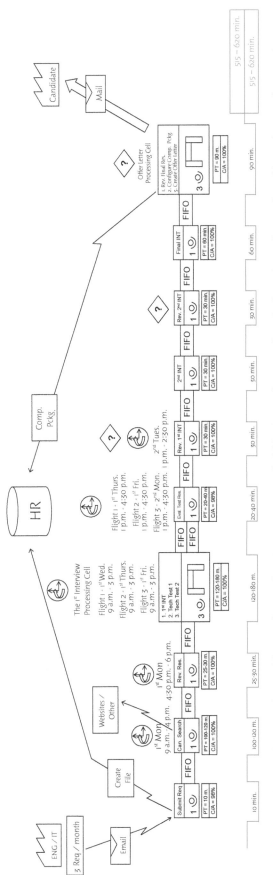

Figure 14.8 In takt capability two, the workflow cycle runs for 90 minutes instead of 30 minutes because there is three times the number of interview results to review.

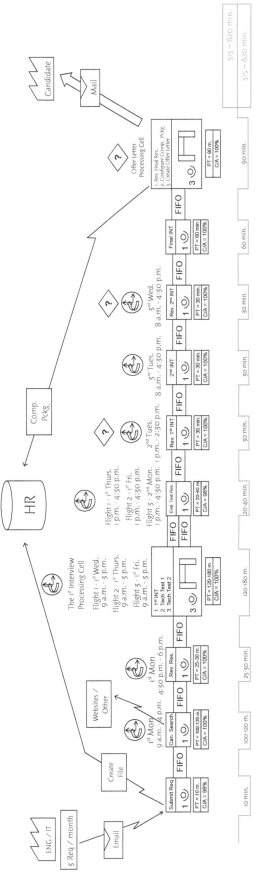

Figure 14.9 All the second interviews can be run on the same day under takt capability two. The results can be reviewed the next day.

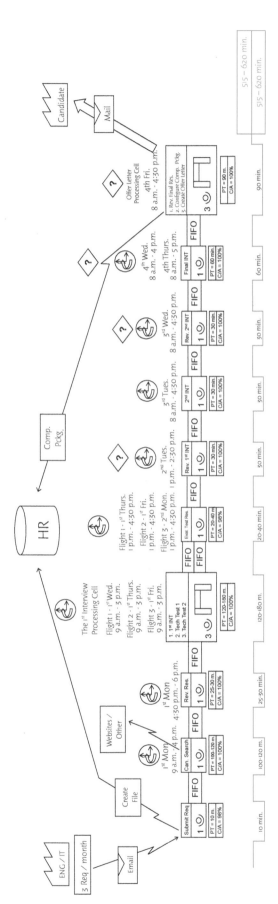

Figure 14.10 The final workflow cycles operating under takt capability two.

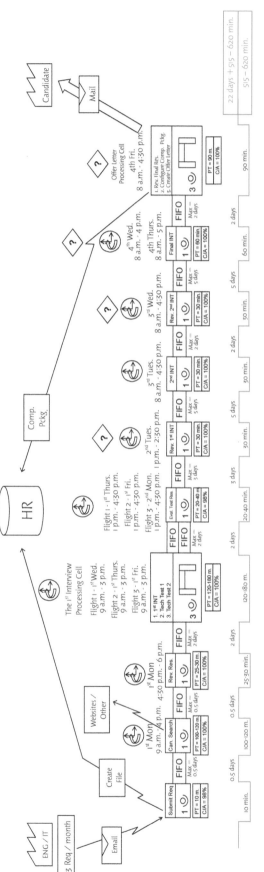

Figure 14.11 The FIFO sizes for the *Technical New Hire* value stream while operating under the higher takt capability.

The *Technical New Hire* GTT under Takt Capability Two

The initialization point will be at the "Submit Request" process. The First Interview Processing Cell, "Second Interview," and "Final Interview" processes will be additional sequencing points.

The GTT begins with "Candidate Search" and ends with the mailing of offer letters to the selected candidates. Pitch would happen at the initialization point, the sequencing points, the processing cells, and also "Candidate Search," because this process marks the beginning of the GTT for the value stream.

The GTT for the value stream is 21.5 days, meaning three new hires could be acquired within the necessary month-long timeframe while operating under takt capability two, compared to being able to hire one candidate per month in takt capability one (Figure 14.12).

practical application | Engineering Changes in Demand

The demand for *Moderate Customer Redesigns* will increase at various points in the year, which means the third takt capability will need to be used (Figure 14.13).

Figure 14.13 **The demand profile for *Moderate Customer Redesigns*, showing the highest takt capability that will be used.**

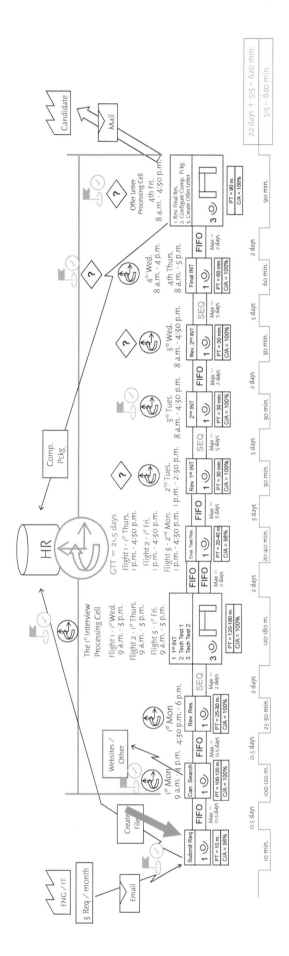

Figure 14.12 While operating under the higher takt capability, the GTT for the *Technical New Hire* value stream is 21.5 days.

During periods of increased demand, the business will need to be able to handle seven *Moderate Customer Redesigns* in a month, which is two more than the takt capability with which we have been previously working.

Similar to Human Resources, we will be able meet this increase in demand under the highest takt capability by running the workflow cycles longer each day. There is enough available time per day to double the length of each workflow cycle and satisfy the conditions of takt capability three (Figure 14.14). A little overtime will be needed for the workflow cycle that takes place on the fourth day. If this is not possible, engineering staff from another department could flex over and help move the work through the value stream.

Sizing FIFO Lanes under Takt Capability Three

With the workflow cycles complete, the FIFO lanes can now be sized for the *Moderate Customer Redesign* value stream. However, the FIFO lane sizes mostly can be the same as they were before, because we had already increased their sizes when they were initially designed to ensure they could hold more than the minimum amount of work required. The sizes of the FIFO lanes before and after the processing cells will be increased slightly, though the FIFO lane feeding "Upload to Ops. DB" can remain at half a day. Because the highest takt capability needs to process seven *Moderate Customer Redesigns* in a month over the normal five per month, increasing the sizes of these FIFO lanes and doubling the length of all the workflow cycles is enough to handle the change in demand (Figure 14.15). While doubling the length of the workflow cycles takes employees away from other tasks, it also ensures that the business is working on its most important priorities.

The *Moderate Customer Redesign* GTT under Takt Capability Three

The GTT for the value stream is 10 days, meaning *Moderate Customer Redesigns* will be fully processed 10 days after "Preliminary Design." The initialization point is at "Receive/Log Req in Database" and there is a sequencing point at "Log Preliminary Drawing." Pitch will be created at the initialization point, the sequencing point, at each processing cell in the value stream, and at "Preliminary Design," since this is the process at which we determine the type of *Customer Redesign* that has come into the business (Figure 14.16). Pitch will also be created at the "Upload to Ops. DB" process, as checking pitch at this process will let us know if the end-to-end flow has been completed on time.

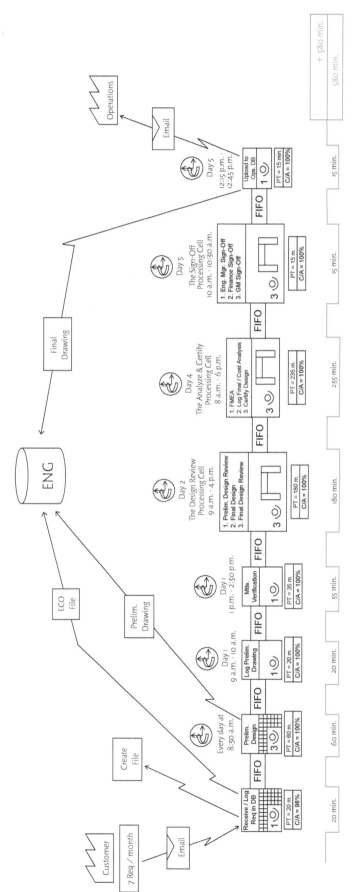

Figure 14.14 By doubling the length of the workflow cycles, we can meet the requirements of the highest takt capability.

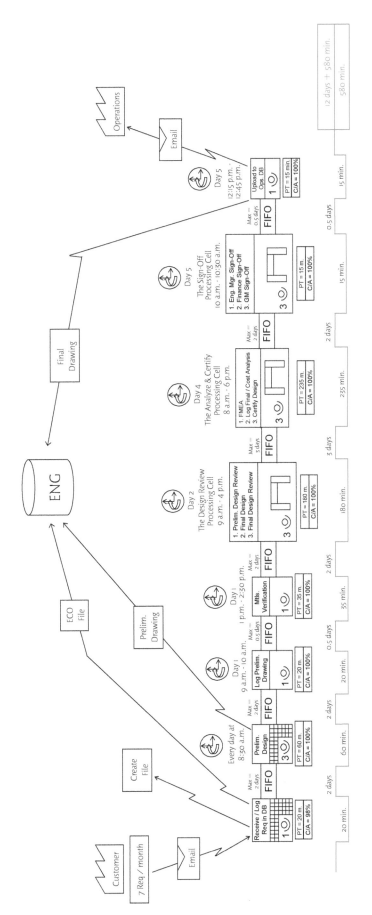

Figure 14.15 **The FIFO lanes sized for the *Moderate Customer Redesign* value stream, operating under the highest takt capability.**

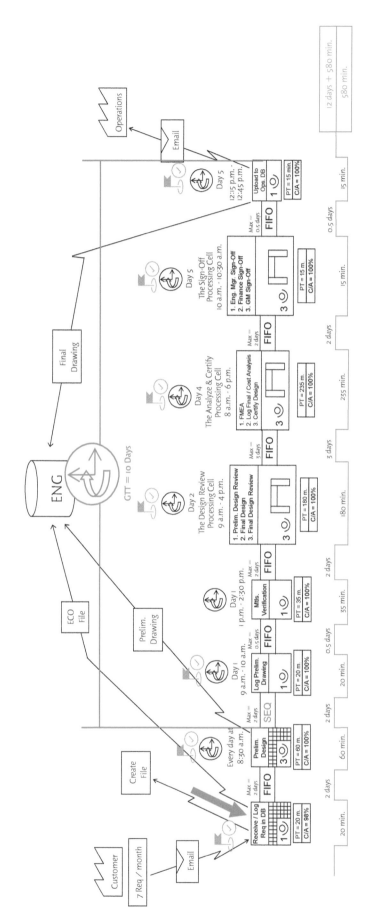

Figure 14.16 The GTT for the *Moderate Customer Redesign* value stream is **10 days.**

Action Item

· ·

Determine how you will handle changes in demand for the value stream.

Check off each step as it is completed.

☐ Determine how changes in demand will be made visual.

☐ Determine how this will happen for digital work.

☐ Establish the process or processing cells at which changes in demand
will be made visual.

☐ Link each takt capability with a specific demand threshold
(if this has not been done already).

☐ Develop standard work for what to do when each demand threshold
is reached.

☐ Before additional takt capabilities are put into use, determine how work
will flow through the value stream from end to end using the nine design
guidelines for office flow.

Acid Test

· ·

Someone from another department can tell if the appropriate amount of work is
being completed just by looking.

Action Item
Create Changes in Demand

Takt capability that will be used

_____
_____
_____

Process or cell at which changes in demand will be made visual

_____
_____
_____

Visual indicators used to convey the need to switch takt capabilities

_____
_____
_____

Visual indicators used for digital work

_____
_____
_____

Standard work for operating under the new takt capability

_____
_____
_____

Notes

_____
_____
_____

chapter
fifteen

Applying the Nine Guidelines:
The Acid Test

The first principle of Operational Excellence is to *Design Lean Value Streams.* This means mapping the current state of how the service gets delivered in the office, then applying the nine guidelines for office flow to that current state in order to design the future state of how the service will be delivered.

Once the future state is generated, it's a good idea to review the future state to ensure the design has been completed to the level it needs to be in order to create flow in the office. Therefore, we should review the future state with the following "acid test" to help ensure the completion of the design.

1. No flow stoppage triangles. These are triangles that represent Uncontrolled Inventory, Waits, and Delays. They would have an "I", "W", and "D" inside them, respectively. These should not exist on a future state map (inventory will still be present, but it will be controlled with FIFO (first in, first out) lanes).

2. All improvement opportunities should be identified. These are commonly called kaizen bursts. One should exist for each of the activities needed to transform the current state into the future state. Wherever there is a difference between a current and future state map there must be a related activity to achieve the change. It should read as: Take the current state and do all of these improvement activities in order to achieve the future state. Therefore, no activity should be missing.

3. The lead time calculations for each FIFO lane should be calculated using the timing of the workflow cycles, not by team consensus or management.

4. A lead time ladder must be present and complete. A value stream map of the office flow is not complete without a lead time ladder that has been correctly calculated.

5. There should be a reduction in lead time. If not, investigate why. Usually, this happens when there was no inventory in the value stream when creating the current state, and no waits or delays were recorded. In these cases, ask if there are waits due to resources not working on this service or delays due to the customer or other external resources (perhaps a supplier). These should be listed in the current state.

6. Processing cells should be used as much as possible. Often, it is thought that there is no application for processing cells. However, work that requires approvals, sign-offs, estimating, getting information to a customer, receiving information from the customer, and any repeatable, transactional activity that requires more than one person should be put into a processing cell if possible. Stretch the imagination here. The benefits are huge.

7. All activities should be formally connected. This means people in a processing cell are connected by passing work to each other, and all other processes are connected through FIFO. There are rare occasions where a supermarket type of connection can exist, but remember that supermarkets mean that we will refill an empty space with the same information that was consumed. In the office, this is indeed rare as we have captured the knowledge, and there is rarely a need to generate the same knowledge or information again. If you believe a supermarket should connect the processes, think in terms of multiple FIFO lanes instead.

8. All workflow cycles should have established times listed. Times such as "As needed" are not a good description of flow, and, in fact, may lead people to believe management will dictate when the workflow cycle will happen, similar to a meeting. Instead, if the workflow cycle is dependent on another event or activity happening first, then we should list the event or activity upon which it is dependent, e.g., a workflow cycle for export orders occurs on Friday at 2 p.m., but only if there are export orders in the FIFO lane.

9. The sequence of the workflow cycles should progress downstream to the end of the value stream to ensure the progression of flow.

10. The point where work is sequenced is clearly identified. This should be a single point, unless the value stream spans across multiple areas of the company and there are natural flow breaks.

11. Where (and, if possible, how) pitch will be applied should be identified. We may not have the exact method we will use to create pitch visually, so it would be okay to list that as an action item on the implementation plan. However, the future state map has to show where pitch will occur.

12. There are no eyeglass symbols, which represent oversight by management, or management intervention.

13. The points where knowledge is formally captured should be identified. Knowledge should also be accessible and shared. Be careful knowledge is not captured on an individual's spreadsheet.

14. Review each process with the five questions for flow. These include:

    1. How do I know what to work on next?

    2. Where do I get my work from?

    3. How long should it take me to perform my work?

    4. Where do I send my work once I'm finished with it?

    5. When I send my work, is flow still normal?

The correct answers to all of these questions should be a single, binary answer. The answers to these questions should not start with "It depends ..."

15. The future state has clearly defined what normal flow for the service will be. We will be able to teach everyone involved how the future state defines normal flow. Any flow outside the parameters shown in the future state will be abnormal flow.

The future state map in Figure 15.1 shows an illustration of a future state map that meets the requirements of the acid test.

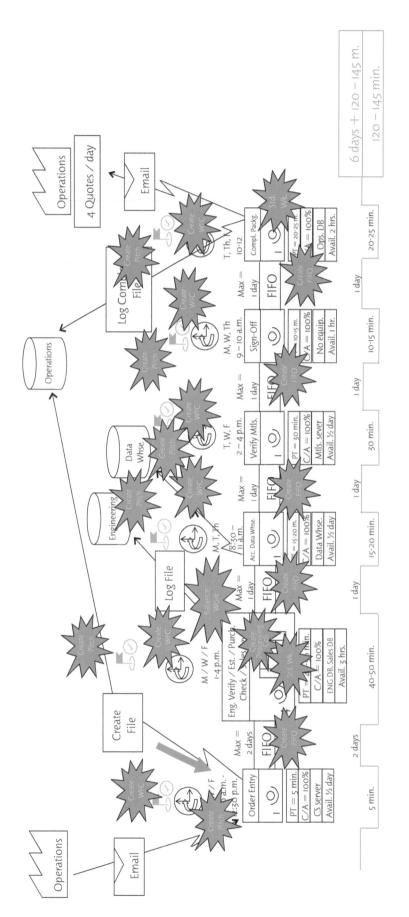

Figure 15.1 **A future state value stream map that passes the acid test.**

practical application   Human Resources
The Acid Test

Let's look at the future state design for the *Technical New Hire* service family (Figure 15.2) and see if it passes the acid test.

1. No flow stoppage triangles: There are none present in the future state.

2. All improvement opportunities should be identified: Kaizen bursts are displayed showing where improvement activities need to happen to generate the future state.

3. The lead time calculations for each FIFO lane should be calculated using the timing of the workflow cycles: This happens in the future state, with extra time buffered in as well.

4. A lead time ladder must be present and complete: This is present in the future state.

5. There should be a reduction in lead time: The lead time has gone from 48 days in the current state to 19.5 days in the future state. The GTT (guaranteed turnaround time) portion of the flow has gone from 25 days in the current state to 16 days in the future state.

6. Processing cells should be used as much as possible: There are two processing cells in the future state.

7. All activities should be formally connected: FIFO lanes connect each processing cell and process together in the future state. There are no informal connections or management oversight.

8. All workflow cycles should have established times listed: All workflow cycles in the future state have established times.

9. The sequence of the workflow cycles should progress downstream to the end of the value stream to ensure the progression of flow: This happens in the future state.

10. The point where work is sequenced is clearly identified: Work is initialized into the value stream at one point, and there are three more sequencing points in the value stream as well.

11. Where (and, if possible, how) pitch will applied should be identified: The future state identifies where pitch will be applied. An action item would need to be developed to explain how pitch will be implemented.

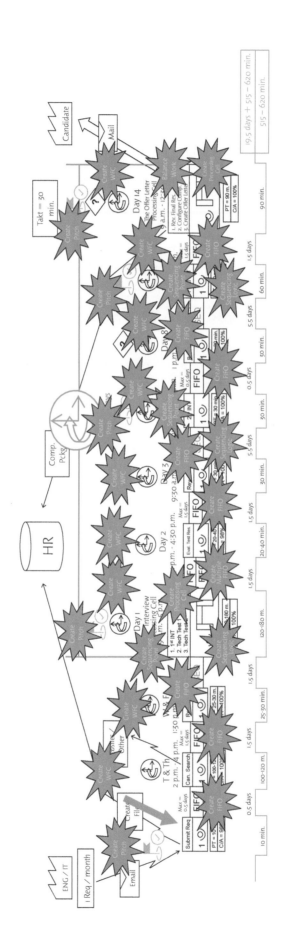

Figure 15.2 The future state flow for the *Technical New Hire* service family.

12. There are no eyeglass symbols: None are present in the future state.

13. The points where knowledge is formally captured should be identified: This is shown on the future state when processes upload information to specific databases.

14. Review each process with the five questions for flow. These include:

    1. How do I know what to work on next?

    2. Where do I get my work from?

    3. How long should it take me to perform my work?

    4. Where do I send my work once I'm finished with it?

    5. When I send my work, is flow still normal?

The correct answers to all of these questions should be a single, binary answer: This is the case for each process and processing cell in the future state.

15. The future state has clearly defined what normal flow for the service will be: This has been done in the future state by providing the GTT and expected delivery of the service provided.

practical application   Engineering The Acid Test

Figure 15.3 shows the future state design for the *Moderate Customer Redesign* service family. We will use the acid test to ensure the future state has applied the guidelines correctly.

1. No flow stoppage triangles: There are none present in the future state.

2. All improvement opportunities should be identified: Kaizen bursts are displayed showing where improvement activities need to happen to create the future state.

3. The lead time calculations for each FIFO lane should be calculated using the timing of the workflow cycles: This happens in the future state, with extra time buffered in as well.

4. A lead time ladder must be present and complete: This is present in the future state.

5. There should be a reduction in lead time: The lead time has gone from 29 days in the current state to 10.5 days in the future state. The GTT portion of the flow has gone from 25 days in the current state to 8.5 days in the future state.

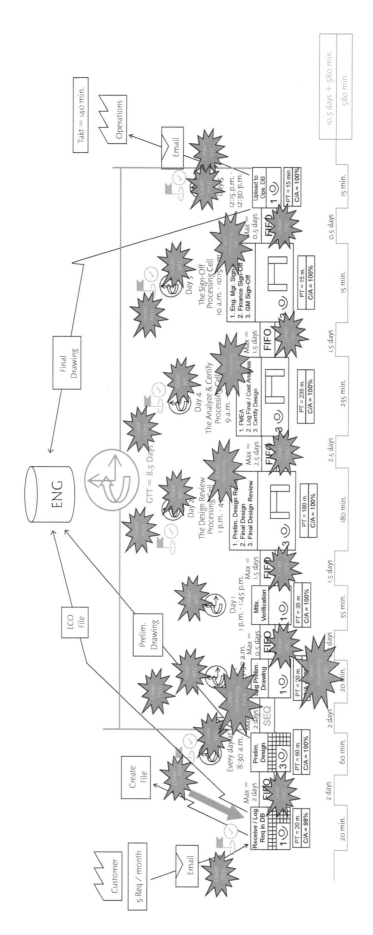

6. Processing cells should be used as much as possible: There are three processing cells in the future state.

7. All activities should be formally connected: FIFO lanes connect each processing cell and process together in the future state. There are no informal connections or management oversight.

8. All workflow cycles should have established times listed: All workflow cycles in the future state have established times.

9. The sequence of the workflow cycles should progress downstream to the end of the value stream to ensure the progression of flow: This happens in the future state.

10. The point where work is sequenced is clearly identified: Work is initialized into the value stream at one point, and there is one more sequencing point in the value stream as well.

11. Where (and, if possible, how) pitch will be applied should be identified: The future state identifies where pitch will be applied. An action item would need to be developed to explain how pitch will be implemented.

12. There are no eyeglass symbols: None are present in the future state.

13. The points where knowledge is formally captured should be identified: This is shown on the future state when processes upload information to specific databases.

14. Review each process with the five questions for flow. These include:

    1. How do I know what to work on next?

    2. Where do I get my work from?

    3. How long should it take me to perform my work?

    4. Where do I send my work once I'm finished with it?

    5. When I send my work, is flow still normal?

The correct answers to all of these questions should be a single, binary answer: This is the case for each process and processing cell in the future state.

15. The future state has clearly defined what normal flow for the service will be: This has been done in the future state by providing the GTT and expected delivery of the service provided.

part
three

Creating Operational Excellence in the Office

chapter
sixteen

Creating Operational Excellence in the Office

As we mentioned in chapter one, traditional Lean attempts to create value stream flow in order to eliminate waste and become more efficient. Operational Excellence requires that we *design* value stream flow (using the nine guidelines) not only to connect processes and set timing to the flow, but with a much deeper intent. The intent of the guidelines is to use methodology and process to establish and define *normal value stream* flow for the service. Understanding what normal value stream flow is to a service is key in achieving Operational Excellence in the office. By defining normal value stream flow, we also define *abnormal value stream flow*. Abnormal value stream flow means something has gone wrong in the flow and it's not working to the design we established. And, no matter how robust the design of our flow is, things *will* go wrong. What we do when things go wrong is the key to achieving Operational Excellence.

Abnormality

Lean initiatives in the office can easily plateau, slide backwards, fall apart, and not have any impact on business growth for one simple reason: *abnormality*. Things go differently than planned, e.g., customer demand becomes erratic, different people do things different ways, work takes longer than expected, interruptions occur, and more. All of these are real-life conditions that occur in the office each day, and they all can cause abnormal flow in the value stream (Figure 16.1).

When an abnormal condition occurs and things don't go as planned, connections in the value stream become broken and flow slows down or stops. Management is alerted and called in. They attempt to give direction on what to do to resolve the issue. However, management direction is not always a

Definition

Abnormal conditions can occur in many places in the value stream

Abnormality is any condition where the design of the value stream flow using the nine guidelines is not functioning as designed.

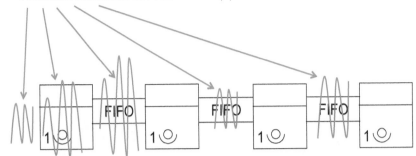

Figure 16.1 **Abnormal conditions can occur at processes or the connections between them.**

quick or correct response to resume flow. Managers have to get information, understand the issue at hand and its effect, and discuss the issue through emails and phone calls with other managers, who may not always be available (Figure 16.2).

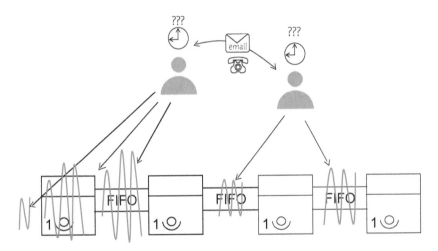

Figure 16.2 **Management tries to handle breakdowns in flow by gathering information and coordinating with other managers in order to make a decision.**

The decision made can have a negative impact on another area of the office. Perhaps the decision does not resolve the issue or everyone is not aware of it. For whatever reason, when the issue does not get resolved and the flow does not resume, management will call a meeting. The intent of the meeting is to resolve the issue, put together an action plan, give everyone the priorities, and get everyone on the same page. In these cases, managers are now spending their time in meetings discussing the lack of performance to the customer, what they will do about it, and what they will say to the customer, which is not a good situation for business growth (Figure 16.3).

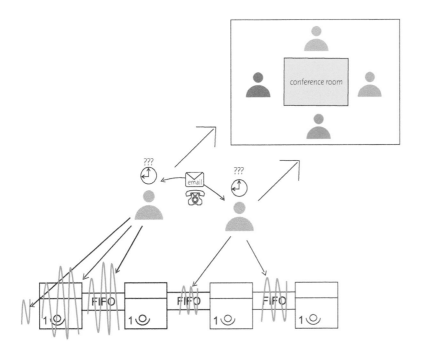

Figure 16.3 **Eventually, managers need to escalate their response to involve multiple managers in a meeting.**

Some companies try to normalize these abnormal conditions by having daily status meetings. Every morning, we meet to discuss the status of where things are, set priorities for the day, and ensure the things management deems necessary are getting done. Although it may seem a good technique to ensure the customer is getting the service, managers are actually embedding themselves into the value stream flow and each day monitoring and adjusting the flow as they see necessary. Each day, managers are attempting to control the flow by overriding the design that was created using the nine guidelines. In these cases, the flow is controlled by management, even if there is nothing wrong with the flow and no abnormal conditions exist. The time spent in these meetings again is not conducive to business growth.

To sum it all up, think of abnormality as follows. Abrnomal conditions:

- Drive management intervention.

- Drive the need for daily or weekly status meetings.

- Drive management to work on defense activities.

- Drive us away from the voice of the customer.

- Detract from our ability to grow the business.

What we do when our value stream flow becomes abnormal counts.

Causes of Abnormal Conditions

Although there can be many causes of abnormal conditions, understanding some of the basic categories can help us understand how to handle abnormalities.

In the office, the major causes of abnormal conditions include the following:

External variation
These are variations that are outside of our control. These could be true demand changes, either by the customer or another area of the company for which the value stream is providing the service. They also could be a different "mix" of work coming into the business, and now we have a number of jobs that take a large amount of time to complete.

Internal variation
These are variations that are within the value stream and within our control, like process variation—the output of the process varies based on who does the work, how the work gets done, or where the work gets done.

External variation is something we need to account for in the design, and we need to be sufficiently flexible to adapt to the service requirements of the customer. The ninth guideline helps us understand this and creates different takt capabilities to handle the external variation.

Internal variations cause disruptions in flow, and here is where efforts can be focused to achieve Operational Excellence. By setting up methods and processes to handle abnormal flow, we can create a barrier around the flow.

Without the need for management intervention, we also can eliminate status meetings and many other meetings as well. The key to handling disruptions in flow is to set up a "self-healing," autonomous flow that corrects itself when things go wrong (Figure 16.4).

Self-Healing, Autonomous Flow in the Office

In practical terms, the real intent of creating Operational Excellence in the office is to create a self-healing, autonomous flow that seamlessly delivers a service to the customer. By self-healing, we mean that when abnormalities occur in the day-to-day operation of the value stream (and they will), the people who perform the work see these abnormalities in the flow and correct them to resume normal flow, all without management intervention.

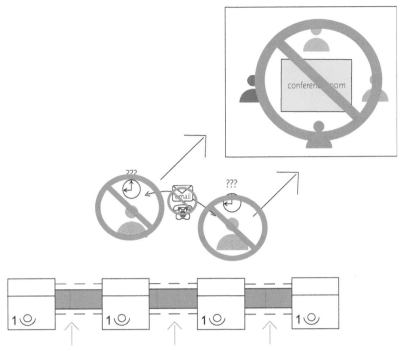

Self-healing flow creates a barrier to prevent management
intervention when there are flow disruptions

Figure 16.4 **Self-healing flow is a barrier that prevents management intervention.**

The guideline here is that no external resource (a supervisor, a manager, etc.)
or event (daily meeting, priority list, conference call) is required to determine
how to resume flow. By autonomous, we mean that this flow happens day in
and day out, by itself. It does not require maintenance or adjustments. It just
works seamlessly each day.

In order to achieve this self-healing autonomous flow, we first have to design
how normal flow will work using the nine guidelines. The nine design guidelines show how information will flow through the office and where we will
capture knowledge. More importantly, the nine guidelines provide us with
a design of flow that we can teach. We can teach how normal flow should
work, how to recognize abnormal flow, and what to do to correct abnormal
flow. With this knowledge, the people who work in the value stream also
understand and can ensure the flow of the service to the customer each
day, autonomously. With the need for management intervention eliminated,
managers can spend their time on activities that grow the business, or
offense activities.

Seeing Abnormal Flow

The first step in fixing abnormal flow is seeing the disruption as it is taking place. This means we need to make the value stream flow in the office visual. To do this, we create visual indicators that show normal versus abnormal flow. These indicators are usually green or red zones in FIFO (first in, first out) lanes, green or red flags that are posted at the end of a workflow cycle, or a physical method for creating pitch that everyone can see. In fact, visual indicators should be placed in the office where a visitor could easily see them just by walking through the office. The idea is that if a visitor can see the visual indicators and know if flow is normal or abnormal, then each employee in the office should be able to tell if flow is normal or abnormal as well.

As mentioned in Chapter 9 on workflow cycles, a key place to put visual indicators is where workflow cycles will take place. A whiteboard for a specified service family can be posted with the respective times for the workflow cycles needed for the family. A green or red token would be present indicating whether each workflow cycle has been completed on time (Figure 16.5).

Accounts Payable Service Families			
Service Family	Workflow Cycle Start Time	Workflow Cycle End Time	On Time?
Expense Reports	8 a.m.	12 p.m.	●
Approvals	8 a.m.	10 a.m.	●
Special Handling	9 a.m.	1 p.m.	●
U.S. Mail	10 a.m.	11:30 a.m.	●
Debits	11:30 a.m.	2:30 p.m.	●
Credits	1 p.m.	3 p.m.	●
Holds	1:30 p.m.	2:30 p.m.	●

Figure 16.5 **A whiteboard can be used to show the different workflow cycle timings for service families in the office and whether they have been completed on time. If red tokens are present, then everyone would know the flow for that service family is abnormal.**

Assigning color codes to the status of flow consistently through the office helps to identify normal and abnormal flow. Normal flow is usually associated with a "green zone," abnormal flow with a "red zone." Sometimes companies also use a "yellow zone" between the two that serves as a warning track. As work backs up, it would progress from the green zone to the yellow zone, which means flow is starting to become abnormal, but we should be able to get it back on track, to the red zone, which means we should do something or customers may be impacted. An easy way to teach when to do something to correct abnormal flow is simply to remember "Red = Reaction." If something is in the red zone, we need to react, and it is the employees who work in the flow who take action, not managers.

Fixing Abnormal Flow

One of the "must haves" in order to create Operational Excellence in the office is *standard work for abnormal flow*. Standard work for abnormal flow means we have established a set of guidelines on what to do if a disruption in flow occurs. When a disruption occurs, it's usually not an easy yes/no decision that will correct the disruption. Several factors typically need to be considered. Therefore, we need to present the standard work in the form that best fits the application. Depending upon the situation, it could be in the form of a checklist, a decision tree flowchart (sometimes referred to as a logic chart), an illustration, or another method. The point is that the standard work leads to a course of action at the end. While it would be nearly impossible to create standard work for all the disruptions that could happen in flow, we should aim at developing standard work for the major disruptions. Yes, there will still be times when management has to step in and assist with guidance, but the goal is to reduce intervention by learning what caused the need for it and adding the response to the existing standard work.

While we have discouraged "brainstorming" or kaizen events to design value stream flow, creating standard work for abnormal conditions is the one place where we would encourage these techniques. We can track the abnormalities as they occur, document them, and then set time aside to have standard work developed to address the issues.

Helpful Hint

While video displays or television monitors can be used to display the information in Figure 16.5, it is important that the people who perform the work be the ones to update the information. If the people performing the work place a red marker on a workflow cycle, then they own it. If someone else tracks it and shows it on a display, then someone else owns it.

Containment Standard Work

When abnormal flow occurs, our standard work should provide the ability to contain the disruption. The containment response should be focused on what needs to happen to keep the flow of information moving. Some guidelines we can follow to help us create containment standard work include:

1. Prevent bad work from entering the flow.

2. Contain the disruptions at the process.

3. If we cannot contain it at the process, then identify workflow cycles where we will "catch up" and designate them as such.

4. Create a "spare" workflow cycle on a different day as an alternate that everyone knows about and can block off time for in order to recover.

5. Provide access to technical assistance.

6. Move the disruption out of the flow.

7. Follow a logic chart with preset responses to limit the spread of abnormal flow.

We'll go into some more detail on each guideline, but they all have in common the aim of catching and containing disruptions.

1. Prevent bad work from entering the flow: Having a checklist of the information needed before the work is initialized at the initialization point or re-introduced at a sequencing point can prevent disruptions from occurring. Information can originate from many different sources, so it's important that all sources have the same checklist. The checklist also should be monitored and improved as new abnormal flow occurrences happen.

2. Contain at the process: We can contain the disruption at a process and not let it move downstream by dedicating more time at the individual process to perform the work, running an existing processing cell longer, or rebalancing work or adding more people to an existing processing

Helpful Hint

In creating standard work for abnormal flow, we are not trying to perform root cause problem solving. Instead, we are accepting that abnormalities will occur in the office and moving to contain them, thus eliminating the need for management intervention.

cell to process work faster. While this would require the employees to put off what they had planned to do and work longer hours on the work needed during the workflow cycle, it also means that the business is working on the right things at the right time. To accommodate this, we might need to extend the FIFO lane to ensure it can hold the extra work required.

3. Identify "catch-up" workflow cycles: When we designate a workflow cycle as a catch-up workflow cycle, then everyone will know that this is the workflow cycle where we will work longer hours or double up on the workflow cycles if needed. The employees can plan their individual calendars accordingly. A simple look at the FIFO lane can tell them they will be working a double on the workflow cycle in Figure 16.6.

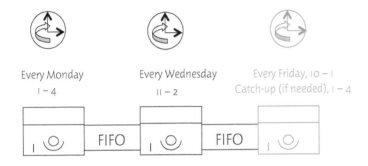

Figure 16.6 **A value stream with an identified catch-up workflow cycle.**

4. Create a "spare" workflow cycle: When we create a spare workflow cycle, we have created a method to contain the disruption from continuing downstream. Having a spare workflow cycle setup can allow us to contain the disruption and not miss important customer dates. For example, if we need to respond to the customer on Friday (as we have established a guaranteed turnaround time with the customer), then a spare workflow cycle could be established on Thursday to make up for any disruptions that may occur (perhaps on Wednesday, we didn't have all the information needed to run the workflow cycle on its normal day). This would ensure that the Friday workflow cycle still takes place as scheduled and that the flow disruption does not negatively impact the customer (Figure 16.7).

Helpful Hint

When management needs to make a decision, the best decisions are ones that focus on the system of flow, what can be done to resume the flow, and what can be done to prevent future breakdowns in the flow.

Figure 16.7 **A spare workflow cycle could take place on Thursday to contain the flow disruption and prevent it from negatively impacting the customer.**

5. Provide access to technical assistance: Another containment resolution could be to physically locate a processing cell near a group of technical support personnel. These support personnel would process their normal work while the processing cell is occurring, but they would be available for questions from the processing cell if needed. These support individuals would not be managers who need to make decisions on what the priorities are, but senior technical employees who provide technical guidance. We would need to make sure they do not schedule meetings during the time at which the processing cell is supposed to run, thus ensuring their availability to help contain flow disruptions. The employees working in the processing cell could simply walk a few steps (or perhaps slide their chair over) to the senior support personnel to ask a technical question, get the answer, and resume the flow (Figure 16.8).

6. Move the disruption out of the flow: If a particular item needs more attention, information from an external source, or more time for research, then we can move this item out of the flow into a "help" location. At the end of the workflow cycle, we can determine the type of help needed, get the help, and resolve some of the more difficult issues related to the item, then put it back into the next workflow cycle. We would also want to document and then address why this occurred and update the standard work so it doesn't happen again.

7. Follow a logic chart with preset responses to limit the spread of abnormal flow: When abnormal flow occurs, we can create a logic chart that dictates the responses to it based on the answers to a series of yes/no questions that contain a preset course of action to rectify an abnormal condition. Both the questions and answers are preset and may change over time as business conditions change. An example of a logic chart is seen in Figure 16.9.

Again, there will be times when management intervention is needed and decisions will be made. Our goal in containment is to limit the number of management interventions and decisions needed.

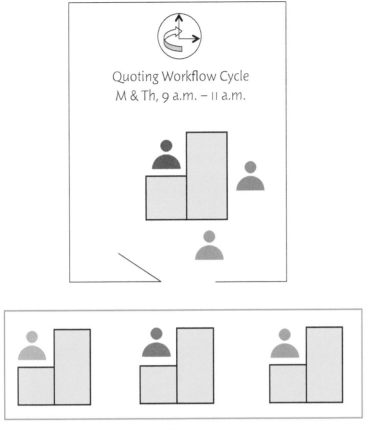

Engineers available for technical assistance

Figure 16.8 **The technical support personnel would be located near the processing cell and be available to assist with questions during the workflow cycle.**

The Office That Has Achieved Operational Excellence

Once we have designed a future state flow using the nine guidelines and created standard work for when flow breaks down, we now have an office that is running on the principles of Operational Excellence. An office that operates on the principles of Operational Excellence would take requests from the customer, process them through its designed value stream, and provide the customer with the information they require on a guaranteed turnaround time, all seamlessly. There would not be any status meetings, setting or resetting of priorities, or chasing down missing or required information. Work would flow to each process, processing cell, and workflow cycle according to the designed value stream flow. Each employee would know if the flow is on time through the visual indicators established and what to do when flow becomes disrupted through the standard work for abnormal flow established.

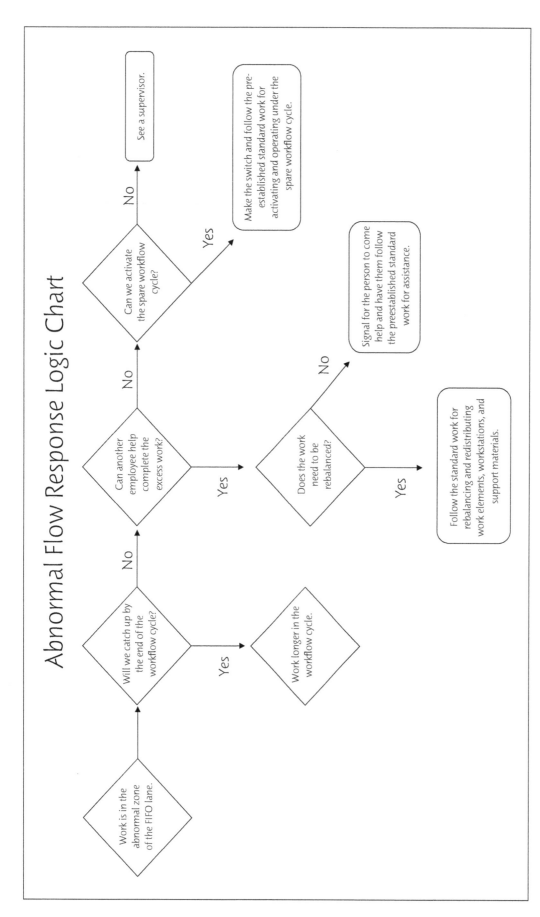

Figure 16.9 **A logic chart that dictates preset responses to abnormal flow conditions based on the answers to a series of yes/no questions.**

Without the need to spend time setting priorities, chasing information, and having meetings to get the service to the customer, the management and senior leadership would be working almost exclusively on offense, or the activities that grow the business. This could involve meeting or talking with customers to inquire about their future business needs and how the organization can provide them with total package solutions to their problems that take work from competitors and gain market share. It would involve working with other divisions on preestablished workflow cycles to plan strategy, and leveraging the capabilities of the organization as a whole for business growth. Management would spend its time listening to customer needs and perhaps even innovating with them.

In an office that runs on the principles of Operational Excellence, they now have the time required to do these things.

Going Forward

The tasks you have just completed in this workbook can guide you on what needs to be implemented in your office to achieve Operational Excellence and make the system of flow designed in these pages a reality. The goal is to achieve Operational Excellence in the office, where, "Each and every employee can see the flow of value to the customer, and fix that flow before it breaks down." Remember to use the nine guidelines for office flow described in this book, and keep Operational Excellence as the destination.

Appendices

Appendix A

Create the Current State Value Stream Map

The process for improving any area of the office proceeds as follows:

1. Determine service families.
2. Create a current state map for each service family.
3. Apply the nine guidelines for office flow.
4. Create the future state.
5. Create an implementation plan.

We covered nos. 1 and 3 in detail, and while several current state maps were developed, we skipped the mechanics of creating them step by step. In this appendix, we will cover current state maps in more detail, as well as define the symbols used. Some of the symbols come from *Learning to See*,[1] some have been modified from that book, and some are new.

Each current state map depicts the flow of one service family. Figure A.1, for example, shows the current state map for a hypothetical "Material Change" and "New Application" service family.

The purpose of a current state map is to achieve credibility and alignment among the members of the organization. With a current state map in hand, everyone agrees that this is how we provide information and capture knowledge in the office, these are the processes and activities that must be completed to deliver our service to the customer, and this is how long it takes to do all of these things.

When creating a current state map, do not aim for perfection. Getting the current state map roughly 75 percent accurate is close enough to begin applying

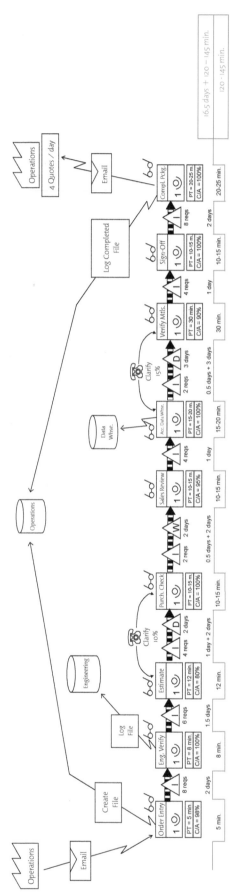

Figure A.1 A current state map for the "New Application" and "Material Change" service family.

the nine guidelines for office flow. Any higher than this, and we will spend too much time trying to get all of the details just right and we will never get on with the implementation. Any less than this and the current state map will not bear enough resemblance to what the office is really like, so we would end up designing a future state flow based on a current state that doesn't really exist.

In a current state map, the flow of information is on the top part of the map and flows from right to left, while the flow of material, knowledge, and the information used by each process to complete its work is on the bottom part and flows from left to right (Figure A.2).

Value stream mapping can be thought of as a language, as different symbols are used to convey different things. Because of this, it is important to follow an agreed upon methodology when constructing current state maps, otherwise people will have different interpretations of what is being shown. The customer symbol, for example, always goes in the upper right-hand corner of *every* current state map. If we were to begin moving this symbol around, people would no longer be able to quickly understand what the current state map was trying to convey.

As the current state map is being created, list any obvious waste inside of a kaizen burst (see below). Note, however, that the way the current state is transformed into the future state is not by eliminating the kaizen bursts via continuous improvement activities, but rather by applying the nine guidelines for office flow. Simply identifying waste on the current state map and then removing it will not achieve Operational Excellence. Along the way to fully applying the nine guidelines for office flow, this waste is usually eliminated, because using the guidelines creates a strict flow that does not allow for much waste to exist.

Below are some of the symbols used in constructing a current state map, as well as what they mean and how they are used.

Customer/supplier (Figure A.3): Who, or what company or entity, initializes the request for the service provided by the office. The same symbol is used for the entity that receives the completed service. The jagged roof indicates that the entity is located outside of the company. Often, though not always, the customer and supplier are the same entity, e.g., a customer requests quotes from us and we send completed quotes back to the same customer. The customer symbol always goes in the upper right-hand corner of the map and the supplier symbol always goes in the upper left-hand corner (there may be more than one of each). List the daily, weekly, or monthly demand under the customer symbol.

Figure A.3

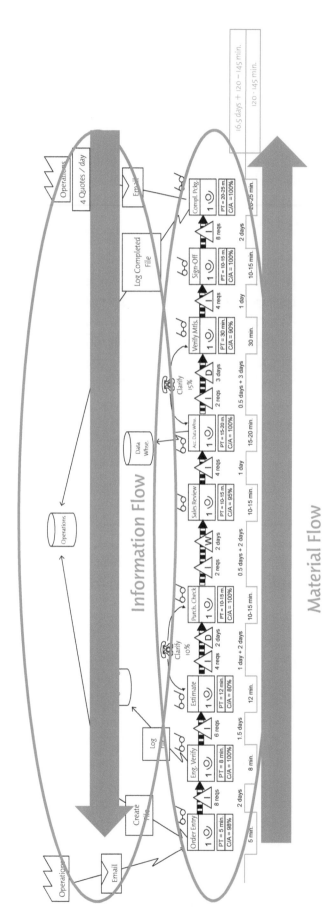

Figure A.2 Information flows from right to left on top, and, on the bottom, material, knowledge, and the information used by each process to complete its work flow from left to right.

Process box (Figure A.4): Defines the boundaries within which a series of activities takes place in flow. The boundaries of the process are defined as where work or information stops and accumulates. Everything in between is considered part of the process.

Employee symbol (Figure A.5): Represents how many employees are needed at a particular process. This symbol goes inside the lower half of the process box, along with the number of employees needed.

Figure A.5

Data box (Figure A.6): Metrics or data that are relevant to the process are captured here. The following data should be listed in each data box: processing time (show the range if one exists; do not take an average), the percent of work that is complete and accurate once it leaves the process (% C/A), any special equipment needed, the number of employees needed, the type of employee needed, the tools or systems required, and how often the employees are available. A data box goes underneath each process box. The process time listed in the data box goes on the lead time ladder for that process.

Figure A.6

Inventory (Figure A.7): Represents inventory that must be processed by a process in the value stream. This inventory could be files, emails, or any other type of work in need of completion, and it might be physically represented at the process or electronic in nature. The amount of inventory present before each process is listed under this symbol. Specifically, this symbol represents *uncontrolled* inventory, which signifies that any amount of work can pile up at a process and more will just keep coming. The inventory amount listed under this symbol goes on the lead time ladder.

Figure A.7

We convert the amount of inventory present at each process into *days worth of inventory* by dividing the amount present at each process by the rate of customer demand per day.

In Figure A.1, for example, the demand is four quotes per day, found under the customer symbol in the upper right-hand corner of the map. If we had four files present before a process, then we would consider this one day worth of inventory. This information would go on the lead time ladder under the process connection.

Figure A.8

Delay (Figure A.8): This is caused by factors outside the company, such as needing clarification from a customer. This symbol would be shown before a process that experiences delays. The length of the delay can be listed as minutes, hours, or days, depending on the unit of measurement required. This number is listed on the lead time ladder.

Figure A.9

Wait (Figure A.9): This is caused by factors inside the company, e.g., an employee not being available, needing additional information, waiting for answers from colleagues, needing to attend meetings, and so on. This symbol would be shown before a process that experiences waiting time. The length of the wait can be listed as minutes, hours, or days, depending on the unit of measurement required. This number is listed on the lead time ladder.

Figure A.10

Push arrow (Figure A.10): Used to indicate when a push system is being used to connect processes. Having a push system means work is completed by one process and pushed to the next person in the value stream *regardless of whether they need it*. If we use push arrows, then it means we also have uncontrolled inventory and should see inventory triangles present, and vice versa.

Figure A.11

Finished goods arrow (Figure A.11): Used to indicate the delivery of the completed service to the customer.

Figure A.12

Manual information flow (paper) (Figure A.12): Used to indicate the flow of information via physical means, such as paper.

Figure A.13

Electronic information flow (paperless) (Figure A.13): Used to indicate the flow of information via electronic or paperless means, such as email.

Figure A.14

"Go See" scheduling (Figure A.14): Signifies management reprioritization at a process. This means that management might reshuffle the desired order of completion for the work that is present, override the expected order of completion, or expedite certain jobs.

Figure A.15

Shared resource process box (Figure A.15): This indicates a process that completes work for more than one service family. Note that we are not talking about the *employee*, just the process. In the office, however, the capabilities of the process are often bound up with the person performing it, so there might not be a difference. The boundaries of a shared resource are defined just like a normal process.

Rework process box (Figure A.16): Indicates that work must flow to a specified process for the correction of mistakes made elsewhere. This is different from two processes simply needing clarification from each other and would be a process that is solely responsible for completing rework in the flow. The boundaries of a rework process are defined just like a normal process.

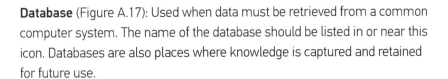

Figure A.16

Database (Figure A.17): Used when data must be retrieved from a common computer system. The name of the database should be listed in or near this icon. Databases are also places where knowledge is captured and retained for future use.

Figure A.17

Decision point (Figure A.18): Indicates that the business needs to make a decision at this point in the flow. Usually, decision points take place at the individual process level. An example of a decision point would be a process or employee deciding whether a candidate continues on in a Human Resources hiring flow.

Figure A.18

Email (Figure A.19): Used when one process communicates to another, or an outside entity, using email.

Figure A.19

Telephone/verbal exchange (Figure A.20): Used to indicate when information is received or transmitted via telephone or in-person conversation.

Figure A.20

Fax (Figure A.21): Indicates when a fax is used to communicate information.

Figure A.21

Regular mail (Figure A.22): Used when one process communicates to another, or an outside entity, using regular mail.

Figure A.22

Kaizen burst (Figure A.23): Signals an identified need for improvement on a current state map. Most kaizen bursts are put on a current state map as a result of applying the nine guidelines for office flow. In other words, when we apply the nine guidelines to a current state map, we recognize that an improvement is needed in order to make the guidelines a reality during the implementation, and this improvement is listed inside the kaizen burst. Completing the work found inside all of the kaizen bursts is what transforms the current state into the future state; it does not happen by identifying waste via kaizen bursts and then eliminating the waste. This will only lead to point-based improvement, not a future state flow designed to achieve Operational Excellence.

Figure A.23

Figure A.24

Figure A.25

Clarification loops (Figure A.24): Shown when processes need to seek clarification from either another process or an outside entity. Be sure to list the typical percentage of work that must be clarified.

Lead time ladder (Figure A.25): Used to evaluate how "Lean" the overall flow is. The bottom of the lead time ladder goes underneath each process box and shows the process time for each process. The top of the lead time ladder goes under the process connection (whatever it may be) and sums all the inventory days, waits, and delays present for that process connection.

At the end of the lead time ladder, a summary is shown comparing the total processing time (the sum of all the bottoms) to the total lead time (the sum of all the tops, plus the total processing time). This summary indicates how long it takes the office to deliver the work that the customer is requesting. There can be a wide range of numbers here, as every office is unique, but it is not uncommon for the total processing time to be several hours or days worth of work and the total lead time to stretch to weeks or even *months*.

Note that the lead time ladder does not compare value-added time to non-value-added time, because there will likely always be some non-value-added time present in the processing time. Each current state map must have a lead ladder, because this is one of the key ways by which we will compare the performance of the current state to that of the future state.

Reference

1.   Rother, M., and J. Shook. 2003. *Learning to See*. Cambridge, MA: The Lean Enterprise Institute.

Appendix B

Create the Future State Value Stream Map

Once service families have been determined and a current state map created, the nine guidelines for office flow are applied to the current state, and this generates the future state.

1. Determine service families.
2. Create a current state map for each service family.
3. Apply the nine guidelines for office flow.
4. Create the future state.
5. Create an implementation plan.

We will now cover future state maps in more detail and also define the symbols used in them. Some of the symbols come from *Learning to See*,[1] some have been modified from that book, and some are new.

Each future state map depicts the flow of one service family and is the result of applying the nine guidelines to that service family and its depiction on a current state map. Figure B.1, for example, shows the future state map for the "Material Change" and "New Application" service family seen in Appendix A.

All the conventions of value stream mapping seen in current state maps still hold true in future state maps: The flow of information is still on the top part of the map and flows from right to left, while the flow of material, knowledge, and the information used by each process to complete its work is on the bottom part of the map and flows from left to right. The customer is still found in the upper right-hand corner of the map and the supplier is still in the upper left-hand corner of the map.

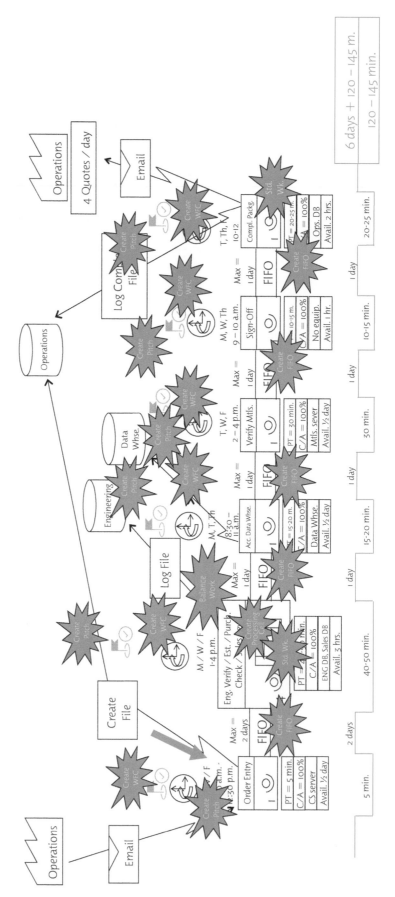

Figure B.1 The future state flow for the "Material Change" and "New Application" value stream.

In the future state, however, there should be no push arrows, inventory triangles, waits, delays, clarification loops, or rework processes (see Chapter 15—The Acid Test—for a more comprehensive list of what should be found on a future state map). It's possible that decision points might still be used. In the Human Resources case study example, the business will still need to make a decision on whether a candidate continues through the hiring process, regardless of whether we are looking at the current state or the future state.

Any kaizen bursts on the future state map should reflect work or improvement activities that need to take place in order to make the future state a reality. Importantly, these kaizen bursts should reflect the work that needs to happen in order to apply the nine guidelines for office flow and then make them a reality in terms of how the office operates.

Similar to the current state, we once again sum the total processing time from the lead time ladder and compare it to the sum of the lead time from the lead time ladder. By applying the design guidelines for office flow, there is usually a significant decrease in the total lead time in the future state when compared with the total lead time in the current state. However, it is not uncommon for there to be no (or a minimal) decrease in the total processing time in the future state when compared with the total processing time in the current state. This is because while the work being done to deliver the service usually does not change that much, the waiting and delays that were common in the current state are usually gone in the future state because the flow required to deliver the service has been streamlined from end to end.

Below are some symbols that are normally used on a future state map. Some of the symbols used on a current state map also are used on a future state map.

FIFO (Figure B.2): FIFO (first in, first out) is used wherever continuous flow (through the use of processing cells) is not possible. FIFO is still a form of flow, because work is moving forward in sequence without priority changes, reroutes, stoppages for meetings, or management decisions. FIFO provides the physical pathway on which information flows *for each service family* between processes. In most office future states, FIFO is a key method to connect processes.

Figure B.2

Workflow cycles (Figure B.3): Workflow cycles refer to work moving through a preset physical pathway at a preset time. They also establish a guaranteed

Figure B.3

turnaround time (GTT) for the flow, which eliminates status checks, phone calls, emails, and the need to chase down information.

Workflow cycles also are critical for ensuring that information flows at predetermined intervals and that knowledge is captured and retained for future use as work proceeds through the value stream. On the future state map, we would note when, on what day, and for how long each workflow cycle occurs to process work. Like FIFO, workflow cycles are very common in most future states.

Figure B.4

Integration events (Figure B.4): Integration events pull a large amount of work forward when the information comes from several different areas of the office and infrequently needs to be moved to another area of the office.

An integration event is also a formal place designated to capture knowledge. This knowledge could be captured in the form of binders, databases, spread-sheets, or many other forms, as long as it is accessible going forward to assist in the processing of future customer requests.

The way an integration event works is that the inputs required by the receiving party are matched with the outputs supplied by the parties providing the information. An integration event is a robust handoff of large chunks of information done such that no follow-up questions, clarifications, redesigns of information, decisions, or overprocessing of information or work are required.

Integration events are not milestone meetings, and no decisions should be made during them.

Figure B.5

Processing cell (Figure B.5): This symbol denotes when multiple activities or processes have been put into either a full-time or part-time continuous flow processing cell. We want to list the names of the processes that occur for the processing cell and the number of employees present. The connected rectangles within the symbol describe how many individual processes or activities take place within the processing cell.

In the data box below this symbol, we would want to note whether the staffing of the processing cell can be staggered or if all employees are needed right when it begins. Generally, it's a good idea to have all employees arrive when the processing cell begins. This way, if questions arise as work is being completed, they can be resolved quickly without compromising the GTT of the cell.

Pitch (Figure B.6): This symbol denotes where pitch is taking place within the office value stream. Typically, pitch is used at the initialization point of the value stream and also wherever there are processing cells. While pitch can be created in many forms, a good pitch will be visual, physical, binary, and anticipated.

Figure B.6

Reference

1. Rother, M., and J. Shook. 2003. *Learning to See*. Cambridge, MA: The Lean Enterprise Institute.

Appendix C
Create the Implementation Plan

The final step in the value stream design process is to create an implementation plan that makes the future state a reality.

1. Determine service families.
2. Create a current state map for each service family.
3. Apply the nine guidelines for office flow.
4. Create the future state.
5. Create an implementation plan.

Part of this step includes normal project planning and tracking techniques, but there are some wrinkles that need to be covered in more detail as we begin to work through how to make the future state come to life in the office.

The main thing to know about constructing implementation plans is that the future state map needs to be broken up into multiple *implementation loops* (Figure C.1).

Breaking up the future state into loops enables the creation of an implementation plan that is easier to manage by taking the totality of work that must be done to make the future state a reality and separating it into different segments, or loops.

Specific sets of tasks then need to be completed in order to make each loop a reality, and these tasks should be what are captured inside the kaizen bursts. The loops seen in Figure C.1 help clarify which tasks and improvement activities, when completed, will translate into making which loop of the future state flow come to life.

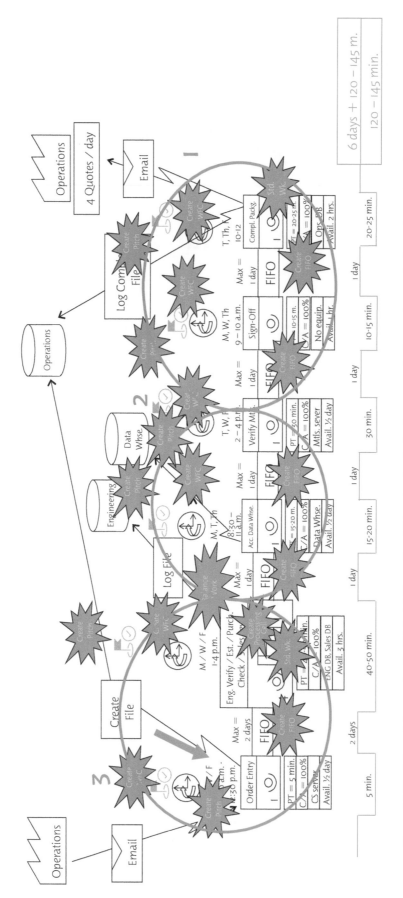

Figure C.1 The future state map for the "Material Change" and "New Application" value stream broken up into multiple implementation loops.

Figure C.2 shows the way these loops would translate to an implementation plan.[1]

By having the kaizen bursts describe what improvement work needs to happen in order to transform the current state into the future state and make it a reality, and by putting this information on the implementation plan by loop, we are able to link together all the steps in the value stream design process. While it's okay to list other kaizen bursts if obvious waste is present and in need of elimination, the intent of the kaizen bursts is to complete them so that the future state might come to life in the office.

Once a future state map has been broken up into loops, it's okay to work on more than one loop at the same time. However, the future state must be "turned on" starting with the loop closest to the customer. In other words, when the office is ready to begin functioning according to the design specified in the future state, the first part of the future state that should begin functioning in this intended manner is the series of processes in the loop closest to the customer.

After this, the rest of the loops can be "turned on" and connected to this first loop by starting with the loop that is next closest to the customer and working backward upstream (from right to left on the map). In Figure C.1, for example, we would need to "turn on" Loop 1 first, then connect it with Loop 2, and then finally connect Loop 3.

With the implementation plan created, the final step of the value stream design process is complete. The next step is to start completing the work described in the implementation plan in order to create an office that functions based on the future state design and the principles of Operational Excellence.

Reference

1.   This implementation plan is based on the model shown in Mike Rother and John Shook. 2003. *Learning to See*. Cambridge, MA: The Lean Enterprise Institute.

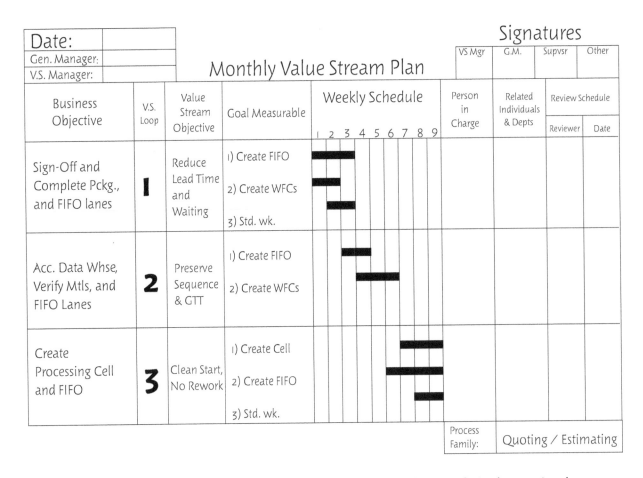

Figure C.2 **Each kaizen burst would be placed as an action item in need of completion on the implementation plan.**

Appendix D

Traditional Lean Techniques to Improve the Office

Traditional Lean applications typically follow the following process:

1. Management sees an area where performance is lacking in the office.

2. A cross-functional team is issued goals and tasked with improving the area.

3. The team creates a current state map that depicts how the office delivers a service to the customer.

4. Opportunities for improvement are identified through kaizen (rapid improvement) bursts.

5. Lean tools, such as kaizen, mistake proofing, problem solving, and others, are used to execute the improvements.

6. Once implemented, the improvements are adopted through standard work.

7. The results are measured and monitored and corrections are made if needed.

8. Management moves on to another area of the office where performance is lacking to begin the cycle again.

In order to improve the area, the traditional approach is to get everyone on the team to "see the waste." To do this, the team creates a current state map of the target area (Figure D.1).

The intent with the current state map is to create agreement and credibility among everyone who works in this area. By walking the office and getting the information from the people who do the work, the map is credible, and it can't be disputed or easily dismissed.

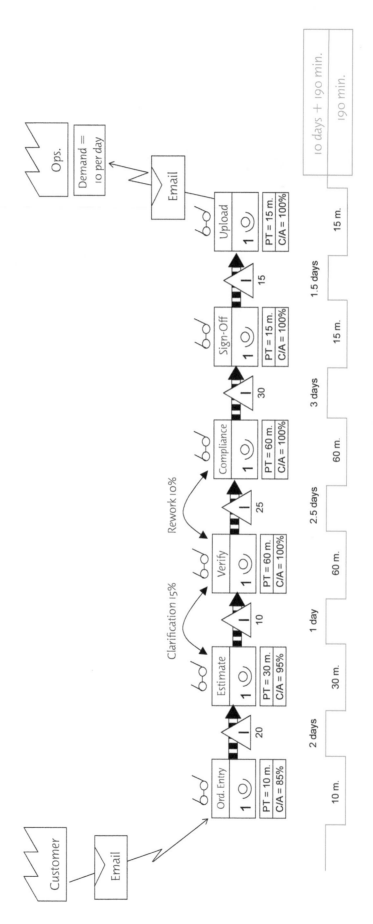

Figure D.1 **A sample current state map.**

Once everyone agrees that the current state map provides a realistic snapshot of the target improvement area, the next step using a traditional approach is to identify opportunities for improvement as seen on the current state map. In Figure D.1, for example, the group might come to an agreement that, in order to achieve the business objective set by management, the approval by the Estimating manager needs to be eliminated since the vice president approves anyway at the "Sign-Off" process.

With this need for improvement established in order to achieve the desired business objective, the team would then place a kaizen burst on the current state map to identify the opportunity for improvement and record the fact that the change needs to be made. It's likely there will be many bursts, because most current states in the office offer significant room for improvement (Figure D.2).

The next step in this process then involves creating project teams to implement each kaizen burst. Specifically, project teams typically run *kaizen events* and use Lean tools during the events to attempt to achieve the goals set by management.

Once the improvements have been made, the team then attempts to sustain the gains made by adopting the new methods through standard work. With standard work established, the team and management then begin to monitor and measure the results to see if the goals are being achieved and what corrections are needed. If all goes well, management selects another area for improvement and the cycle starts again with a new team.

This traditional approach differs from Operational Excellence in an important way: There is no design, process, or methodology followed when improvements are made in the office. Operational Excellence designs flow from end to end using principles and guidelines, which defines normal and abnormal flow, then makes those flow conditions visible to everyone working in the office. The end result is that the office can be leveraged for business growth because employees, not managers, are capable of fixing the flow before it breaks down. Management spends its time not chasing emails, voicemails, and holding meetings, but rather working on the activities that grow the business, or offense.

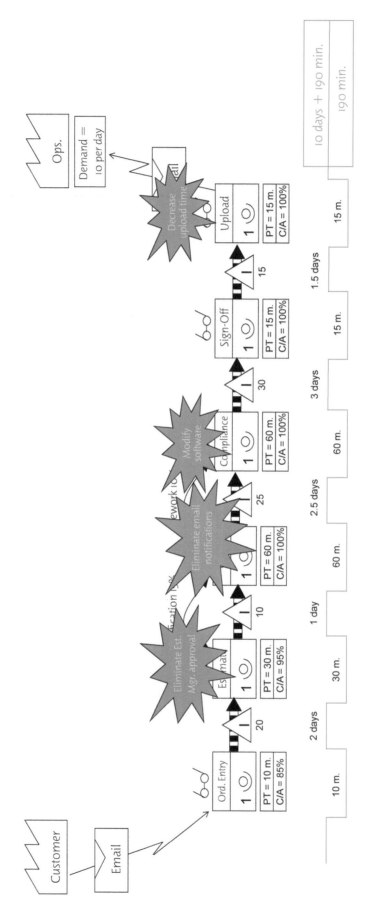

Figure D.2 A sample current state map showing multiple kaizen bursts, each of which denotes an opportunity for improvement that must be made to achieve the management-defined business objective.

Appendix E
The Lean Plateau

After years of continuous improvement performed by seeking out areas to eliminate waste, the low-hanging fruit evaporates. Eventually, the improvements begin to stumble over each other; a positive improvement in one area negatively impacts an improvement in another. Over time, many companies have found that their continuous improvement initiatives usually reach a point of diminishing returns and eventually plateau (Figure E.1).

The plateau could occur not only because the low-hanging fruit is gone. There are many other factors as well. Stress in the ranks of management may occur because improvements that have big impacts (like the initial ones) become harder to find, or they constantly have to be negotiated with other managers on why their improvements are not good for them. Changes in management occur, too.

Perhaps the leader who drove and supported the improvement efforts has moved on to a new company, or other business needs took his/her attention away. There are many other reasons why some companies reach a plateau or even slide backward as momentum declines (Figure E.2).

One of the most prevailing reasons why companies hit a Lean plateau is simply the fact that traditional Lean considers continuous improvement to be a never-ending journey; eliminating waste is a never-ending journey. However, that journey does not always go in the same direction. It also can split off into different directions, and it can happen at different speeds.

In short, the reason many companies plateau along their continuous improvement journey is because

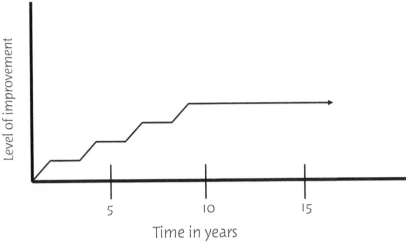

Figure E.1 **The Lean plateau.**

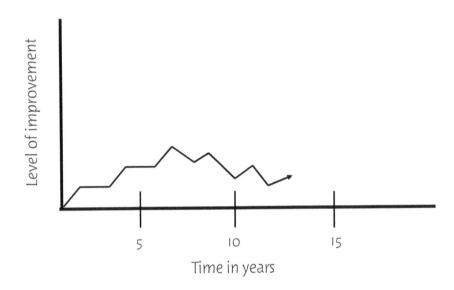

Figure E.2 **It's possible to slide backward on the continuous improvement journey, losing progress that took years to achieve.**

they do not have a destination for the totality of their improvement efforts, and, instead, believe the intent is to continually eliminate waste and get a little better each day.

Setting a destination of Operational Excellence prevents companies from hitting the Lean plateau. By recognizing that end-to-end flow must be designed following principles and guidelines, organizations ensure they avoid the Lean plateau by understanding the intent of all of their improvement efforts, which is to get the office to a place where, "Each and every employee can see the flow of value to the customer, and fix that flow before it breaks down"—the very definition of Operational Excellence.

Index

root cause problem solving, 224

S

"Schedule with Divisional Project Planning" activity, 24
scheduling, 116–117, 157
scope and scoping
    Engineering application, 33–37
    Human Resources application, 27–32
    service families, 20–22
"Second Interview" activity, 173, 197
self-healing, autonomous flow, 220–221
self-healing value streams, 5
sequencing and sequencing points
    acid test, 207, 209, 213
    FIFO, 95–96
    multiple candidate positions, 129
    potential disruption, 173
    single-point initialization, 168–171
    single-point initialization guideline, 168, 173
service families, *see also specific family*
    acid test, 39
    action items, 38–41
    common traits trap, 28
    current state value stream map, 15, 43–47
    defined, 20
    description, 41
    determination, 15, 19–41
    80/30 guideline, 24–27
    electronic creation, 24
    engineering application, 33–37
    human resources application, 27–32
    identities, 30
    multiple, 99–100
    names, 30
    overview, 15, 17
    refining the scope, 22–24
    scoping the matrix, 20–22
    steps checklist, 38
    value streams, 27
    work content range, 53
shared resource process box symbol, 238
"Sign Off" activity

Y